'I think globally, but I spend locally.'

Think Globally, Spend Locally
The Illustrated Guide to Globalization

Christopher Arnander

PRO

First published in Great Britain in 2003 by
Profile Books Ltd
58a Hatton Garden
London EC1N 8LX
www.profilebooks.co.uk

10 9 8 7 6 5 4 3 2 1

A CIP catalogue record for this book is available from the British Library.

ISBN 1 86197 653 4

Designed and typeset in Korinna by MacGuru Ltd
info@macguru.org.uk

Printed and bound in Great Britain by
Bookmarque Ltd, Croydon, Surrey

Contents

'Grab some lederhosen, Sutfin. We're about to climb aboard the
globalization bandwagon.'

'They'd soon change their tune if they'd ever flown business class,
stayed in four-star hotels, all on expenses …'

INTRODUCTION

I have always thought it rather quaint that my trusty old dictionary of 1972 should be called *The Shorter English Dictionary*. After all, it comes in two massive volumes and seems to include every word that might be of interest to me; what can the unshortened work be like? Yet 'globalization' – whether spelt with 's' or 'z' – is nowhere to be found.

Today, globalization has become the burning topic of the hour. The media are full of it; its opponents and proponents clash in the streets. One internet bookshop lists over 1,200 books on the subject, many with provocative titles, such as *Amoral Elephant*, *Unruly World* or *Losing Control*. More than seventy books have titles beginning *Globalization and...*

So what is globalization? The word originally meant no more than the worldwide spreading of something, but it has come to be an ambiguous buzzword applied to a wide range of human endeavour. Above all, it denotes the Anglo-Saxon capitalist system; rooted in 16th-century England, this system was transplanted across the ocean and helped fuel America's almost uninterrupted rise to global leadership over the last 150 years.

From the command economies of the early fifties to the unbridled capitalism of today, *Think Globally, Spend Locally* offers a cartoonist's insight into the trials, tribulations and foibles of the business world, in an increasingly global environment. The cartoons speak for themselves, but comment and chronology help to set their context.

The first multinational

'Out of the abundance of fruit which some region enjoyeth, the necessitie or wante of others should be supplied'; with these words, Queen Elizabeth I of England launched the East India Company, when she gave it its Royal Charter on the last day of 1600. They could almost find a home in the mission statement of the World Trade Organization (WTO).

The East India Company was the greatest of the joint stock companies that built the British Empire; it could justly claim to be the first multinational, though it was for some decades outshone by a Dutch lookalike. The company structure gave continuity and helped England (not yet united with

Scotland) to steal a march on its Spanish and Portuguese competitors globally. An early specimen was the Virginia Company, named after the Virgin Queen Elizabeth; its colony was to be the breeding ground for four of the first five US presidents.

The Tudor and Stuart joint stock companies were the direct ancestors of today's limited liability company. They foreshadowed the great privatization fashion that is sweeping the globe today. The monarch delegated to the private sector projects which he or she could not carry out, hoping to gain political or monetary benefits from them and avoid the risk of reputational damage. It was also an early form of off-balance-sheet financing.

There's nothing new under the sun

When the Bank of England was founded in 1694, many features of today's Anglo-Saxon capitalism were already present in London – mostly borrowed from Amsterdam: trading in shares and derivatives; regular stock manias; honest, as well as dodgy, company promotions; the quest for good (and, preferably, inside) information; an embryonic central bank – there were even laws 'to restrain the number and ill practice of brokers and stockjobbers'. Above all, there was Britain's government bond market – the mother of all bond markets – which financed the global expansion of empire.

Then Britain seized market leadership in the slave trade. Slaves were sent over the Atlantic to work in Caribbean and American plantations, which sent sugar, tobacco and cotton to England, which in turn sent commodities and artefacts to Africa to pay for the slaves. Having thrived on this nefarious trade, Britain, to its credit, abolished it; there is, officially, no slavery today, but global companies are just as interested as the slave owners of old in reducing staff costs, often by moving manufacture to a low-cost country. Best not to ask if your coffee or carpet could have been made by young children working as slaves …

The Declaration of Independence in 1776 cost Britain 13 colonies, but it could now become the workshop of the world and consolidate a global empire 'on which the sun never sets'. The 19th century saw the prototype of globalization as we know it – the dissemination of finance, industry, trade, knowledge, culture, language, people, laws and religion across borders. Britain was the leader, with America, other European countries and Japan joining the party after 1860. The thrust of globalization today is similar to what it was then, even if it is now enforced by bureaucrats of the World Trade Organization rather than the fusiliers of the British crown.

Globalization was stopped in its tracks by the weight of two world wars, hyper-inflation, revolution, protectionism and depression; the British Empire faded away. Then came the Marshall Plan in Europe and the American reconstruction of Japan. The scene was set for Anglo-Saxon capitalism to resume its global surge, but now under American leadership. It was slow at first but became a flood after the two oil shocks, the advent of Margaret Thatcher and Ronald Reagan, and the fall of the Soviet empire.

Mickey Mouse goes global

Many of the cartoons chosen to illustrate globalization in these pages are wonderfully absurd, yet full of sharp insights.

'And, finally, after a day of record trading on Wall Street, the entire world was owned by Mickey Mouse,' says a TV announcer. One thinks of the global spread of Hollywood culture, as well as the manic merger and acquisition binge that has reduced many fine old companies to Mickey Mouse status.

When the chairman of the board says to the sole woman director: 'That's an excellent suggestion, Miss Triggs. Perhaps one of the men here would like to make it?' we are reminded of the stubborn reluctance of some men to admit that women have anything to offer in business, despite laws giving equal rights for women nearly everywhere.

Some of the cartoons need no words. David Langdon perfectly captures Margaret Thatcher's expression when, regaled as Britannia, she reluctantly accepts British participation in the Exchange Rate Mechanism in 1989. The ensuing imbroglio led to her loss of office but her instinct about the ERM was spot on.

Emma Lazarus wrote a poem for inscription on the Statue of Liberty, which was opened in 1886; it has been the inspiration for millions of immigrants to America:

3

Give me your tired, your poor,
Your huddled masses yearning to be free,
The wretched refuse of your teeming shore,
Send these, the homeless, tempest-tost to me,
I lift my lamp beside the golden door.

They are marvellous words, but the cartoonist JB Handelsman imagines the Statue saying into her mobile phone: 'Well, it all depends. Where are those huddled masses coming from?'

If they are from what Shakespeare might have called 'less happier lands' – the emerging markets – we may not have room for them, though, of course, we would like them to go on absorbing our investments, goods and culture. There really must be some limits to free trade!

It won't end in my time

Old George Brudenell was an English country squire, who happened to live his life at least a century after his natural time. His heart was at Balaklava, where his ancestor had led the Charge of the Light Brigade. In the 1950s he still wore a frock coat, spats and a top hat. He fretted at all the new-fangled things, such as electricity, cars, radios, telephones and television. 'I don't know where it's all going to end,' he said gloomily one day, as he stared out over his land, adding: 'What's certain is that it won't end in my time.'

Where is globalization taking the human race? Its supporters, such as the IMF, can justifiably point to 'unprecedented gains in human welfare' across the globe, particularly for nations that are good at trading. At the same time, its detractors are passionately convinced of its drawbacks; typical of them were the Mexican peasants who launched a violent revolt against trade liberalization in 1994, with the cry that it was 'a death certificate for the indigenous peoples'. Whatever one's view, a number of major issues must be resolved in the early years of the 21st century.

Capitalism's animal spirits showed signs of getting out of hand. Enron proudly claimed to be 'laser-focused on earnings per share', but its lies about those earnings led one of the world's biggest companies to bankruptcy and disgrace. Many other companies had cooked the books, often supported by errant accountants and bankers; numerous corporate leaders

'I hear we've just been granted most-favoured-nation status.'

were caught looting their companies or being secretly paid far beyond the dreams of avarice. Could capitalism get over the blow to its credibility and clean up its act?

Five East Asian nations received $93 billion of hot money in 1996 and lost $105 billion in 1997 – a huge setback after years of success for these 'tiger' economies. Russia suffered similarly from hot money flows; with its gross domestic product down 50% in the space of a decade, many Russians looked back nostalgically to the communist era. Then Argentina, potentially so wealthy and seemingly a model pupil in the IMF kindergarten, completely collapsed. Might there be flaws in the Anglo-Saxon liberal capitalist model, with its accent on free flows of money across the exchanges? And what could be done about corrosive corruption, which often flourished more vigorously in the new democracies than in the old tyrannies?

Twenty-two thousand delegates, and numberless camp followers, attended the Earth Summit in Johannesburg in 2002, but governments seemed unable to take the steps needed to protect the environment. There was a whole panoply of seemingly unsolvable problems – desertification, erosion, falling fish stocks, species disappearance, forest loss, climate change and general ecological decline. These problems are hard to address because of the essential short-termism of most of the human race, not least our political masters – as a British Prime Minister, Harold Wilson, once said: 'A week in politics is a long time.' Most of us cannot see the ozone depleting or the desert spreading so why clutter up our minds with such things?

But globalization certainly seems to be unstoppable, whether for good or for bad. And we can readily agree with George Brudenell that it won't end in our time.

'Right there near the missile site. Isn't he the Russian we always bump into at the Geneva Disarmament Conference?'

A HEDGEHOG IN UNCLE SAM'S PANTS, 1951–72

After World War II came a new nightmare – the Cold War. Globalization had reached its peak in 1914 but would have to wait a little longer before surging again. America rebuilt friend and foe alike but the scope for international business was limited at first; wartime controls prevailed and entrepreneurs felt unloved.

Then, in the early fifties, a few straws in the wind pointed to the hurricane of globalization to come. In the UK and USA, the Tories and Republicans returned to power; they were more friendly to business and inclined (though scarcely able) to reduce taxes and regulations. In Moscow, Stalin's death suggested a thaw in East–West relations, but the thaw was regularly interrupted by events such as the Hungarian Revolution or Khrushchev's provocative placing of nuclear missiles in Cuba. 'Why don't we throw a hedgehog down Uncle Sam's pants?' he asked, thereby almost provoking a nuclear war. The long Vietnam tragedy and the arms race only made matters worse.

Out of a blue sky, the Eurocurrency market was born; at first, it was a tiny device for communist regimes – fearful of confiscation – to keep dollars out of America's clutches, but it grew into a loosely regulated and widely used leviathan, a major plank of globalization. Another plank was trade, which grew at twice the speed of economic output, as the world couldn't get enough of US goods and Japan, Germany and Italy, defeated in war, created export-based miracles.

By the early seventies, superpower rearmament had achieved mutually assured destruction ('MAD'); it was time for Soviet–American détente and for bringing China on board. Then, rather to everyone's surprise, a nasty turn of events in the Middle East knocked the global economy off course, after two decades of growth.

'The basic problem Carstairs, is this – how to uphold the best traditions of gunboat diplomacy with a singleton in gunboats.'

REDUCTIO AD ABSURDUM
'We'll soon have you fighting fit.'

MR MACMILLAN: 'It's not my duty to go about stopping people doing things.'

1951

FREEING THE PEOPLE

Britain had lost an empire, but not yet found a role, as US statesman Dean Acheson was to tell the students of West Point; the people turned to a Labour government more interested in domestic revolution than in imperial grandeur.

A much weakened Britain was 'punching above its weight' overseas. In April 1951, the Korean War was raging and more money was needed; then Britain was building an atomic bomb – 'we've got to put the bloody Union Jack on top of it', Foreign Secretary Ernest Bevin had said. So the Labour Chancellor, Hugh Gaitskell, raised corporate and personal taxes and then proposed a dividend freeze, which threw the Stock Exchange into 'complete disorder'. People were getting fed up with the nanny state and wanted change. In October, the Tories, under Winston Churchill, were back in power, on a promise to 'free the people'. The Housing Minister, Harold Macmillan, encouraged the private sector with a pledge to build 300,000 houses, though he faced parliamentary criticism for allowing a tall building to overshadow St Paul's Cathedral.

Children were delighted by the end of sweet rationing; business morale was lifted by the new *laissez-faire* attitude of the Tories after six years of controls, but Britain's weak financial and economic situation stifled any nostalgia for its 19th-century global leadership. Regulations and taxes remained oppressive; exchange control was particularly damaging to London's role as the major global trading and finance centre.

AND...

Political & general

Apr President Truman dismisses MacArthur, US Pacific army chief, for insubordination.
May UK diplomats, Burgess and MacLean, defect to Soviet Union. Festival of Britain boosts UK's morale as post-war recovery gathers pace.
Sep Japan signs peace treaty with 49 nations, excluding Soviet Union. China occupies Tibet.
Oct Conservatives win election; aim to privatize industries nationalized by Labour and reduce controls over business.
Dec Libya independent (colonized by Italy in 1911).

Business & finance

Japan Development Bank founded; Japan's economy grows 10% per annum in next two decades.
Mar Nationalization of foreign oil interests in Iran. First commercial computer, Remington Rand's UNIVAC, for US Census Bureau.
Oct First US coast-to-coast dialled phone service.
Dec Conservatives use Bank Rate to control inflation in UK, after it had remained unchanged at 2% for 12 years. First effective production of electricity from atomic energy, Idaho, USA.

1952

GOOD FOR GENERAL MOTORS

In the early months of 1952, Republicans courted the World War II hero, General Dwight D Eisenhower. He was the Supreme Commander of the allied forces in Europe and would be an ideal presidential candidate. Who better to deal with the Korean War and the Soviet threat? Who better to control US military expenditure, which was surging towards $50 billion a year? In June, he finally took the plunge and resigned from the army; everyone liked Ike and he went on to win the election, succeeding Harry Truman and bringing Richard Nixon along on his coat tails as vice president.

Charles Wilson, the General Motors boss, became Defense Secretary. His remark that 'what was good for our country was good for General Motors and vice versa' was often maliciously misquoted in its vice versa form, but it suggested a White House that would support business – at least, big business. It wasn't long before wage and price controls were lifted, but the Cold War did not allow much reduction in military spending or taxes.

Europe's victors, vanquished and neutrals were gradually recovering from war, aided by the timely and generous injection of $13 billion from the Marshall Plan. Under America's tutelage, Japan was starting a miraculous era. A century previously, it had been America's 'manifest destiny' to conquer a continent; now it was time to climb aboard the globalization bandwagon and conquer the world by peaceful means.

AND...

Political & general

Jan First general election in independent India; Pandit Nehru premier.
Feb Death of UK's King George VI, succeeded by Queen Elizabeth II.
Jul After anti-British riots in Egypt, military ends monarchy. Rise of Col Gamal Abdel Nasser.
Oct At 19th Party Congress Stalin discusses imposition of communism in Western Europe. In Kenya, Mau Mau (nationalist movement) violently resists UK colonial rule.
Nov First UK atomic bomb; first US hydrogen bomb.
Dec London smog kills 4,000; Clean Air Act to reduce pollution passed in 1956.

Business & finance

Jun Confidence returns to UK stock market, which doubles over next 3 years and rises more than 3 times over the next 12 years.
Sep European Steel & Coal Community in force. Conservatives announce plan to privatize steel industry.

'You blow a billion here, you blow a billion there. It adds up.'

'All during the Stalin years, Alexei, your father managed,
secretly, to keep Soviet tap dancing alive.'

'Dear Mr Malenkov – While you seem to be in receptive mood, may I refer to some Imperial Redeemables purchased in 1910?'

1953

A THAW IN THE EAST

'All Russia wept,' said the poet Yevgeny Yevtushenko, when Joseph Stalin died in March 1953. Despite being a ruthless dictator over a quarter of a century, Stalin was loved and respected by many of his people. To the rest of the world his death indicated a possible thaw in the East.

The new man, Georgi Malenkov, looked friendly and receptive enough, although he had been up to his neck in the great purges of the thirties; within two years, he was elbowed aside by the jovial and mercurial Nikita Khrushchev and sent to run a power station in Kazakhstan – no doubt a better fate than he would have endured under Stalin. The Soviet people and the wider world soon found out that there was no real thaw; internal suppression, cultural conformity and external hostility continued as before, though applied more erratically. Universal terror became *à la carte* terror.

Monolithic state organs controlled all trade and industry and entrepreneurial activity could cost you a jail sentence, if not your life. It would be another 20 years before the beginnings of a Soviet engagement with the global economy, while Imperial Russian bond holders would have to await the fall of the Soviet Union to get a settlement.

AND...

Political & general

Jan Dwight Eisenhower President, Richard Nixon Vice President of USA.

Mar After Stalin's death, Soviet army quells revolt in East Germany; other satellites in turmoil.

Apr DNA structure published (Watson and Crick).

May Mount Everest climbed by Hillary and Tensing.

Jul Korean War ends after 5 million lives lost; stalemate between the two Koreas at previous borders.

Aug First Soviet hydrogen bomb. Failed coup in Iran strengthens Shah's position.

Oct Central African Federation set up – precursor of Zambia, Malawi and Zimbabwe.

Dec Death of Ibn Saud, founder of Saudi Arabia.

Business & finance

Jan Charles Clore makes first post-war hostile takeover in UK – the Sears shoe shop chain, which had hidden real estate values.

Mar British aircraft industry stunned as world's first jet airliner, Comet, has four crashes in two years (metal fatigue).

Oct United Steel Companies becomes first of 8 UK steel companies to be denationalized.

Dec UK Housing Minister Macmillan celebrates annual building of 300,000 houses as 'a triumph of private enterprise'. George Marshall awarded Nobel Peace Prize for economic reconstruction of Europe; his plan injected $13.3 billion into 16 nations.

'I could have bought General Motors in 1949 for twenty-six dollars a share. I could have bought Boeing for six dollars a share. I could have bought Electric Boat for thirteen dollars a share. I could have …'

1954

MISSING THE BOAT

Nothing is more annoying than missing a good buying opportunity or selling too soon, but the old investor had particular cause to feel frustrated; Electric Boat shares had risen 60 times in five years, boosted by Cold War defence expenditure, and he had missed the rise, as the company – builder of the atomic powered submarine *Nautilus* – became transformed into the excitingly named military contractor General Dynamics. But if he had got up from his analyst's couch that winter day in 1954 and bought the shares comprising the Dow Jones Industrial Index, his grandchildren might have been sitting on a nest egg worth 20 times what he paid.

Or did his grandchildren perhaps succumb to one of the stock market manias that regularly distort the capitalist system? Did they throw out their 'old economy' stocks in favour of the latest fad, be it conglomerates, dotcom companies or emerging market equities?

Open equity markets are the distinct mark of Anglo-Saxon capitalism; other successful nations have relied on more limited and opaque equity markets to achieve growth. At the end of the 20th century, the Anglo-Saxon cult of the equity seemed to be sweeping all before it, but the new century opened badly as markets fell for three years in a row, weakening economic performance.

AND...

Political & general

Mar Dr Jonas Salk's polio vaccine licensed for use in USA.
Apr Nasser takes power in Egypt.
May French surrender at Dien Bien Phu; Ho Chi Minh assumes power in North Vietnam, while South Vietnam is supported by USA – seeds of future Vietnam War. US Supreme Court finds segregation unlawful.
Jun CIA sponsors coup in Guatemala.
Jul Food rationing ends in UK.
Sep South East Asia Treaty Organization set up by USA, UK and Pacific countries against communist threat.
Oct France sends 20,000 troops to quell revolt in Algeria.
Dec Senator Joseph McCarthy censured for 'conduct unbecoming a senator' after witch-hunt against the US Army.

Business & finance

Mar Re-opening of gold market boosts London's role as global financial centre.
May Texas Instruments announces production of silicon transistors.
Jul Debut of first US passenger jet, Boeing 707.
Nov Partial deregulation of London's international art market; antiques and works of art able to be imported, despite severe exchange controls generally.
Dec Anglo-Iranian Oil Company renamed British Petroleum, after nationalization of Iranian assets.

*'I sold my soul for about a tenth of what the
damn things are going for now.'*

'Not you, Charlie.'

'One thing's for sure.
The First National Bank will never forgive my my trespasses.'

1955

NEW YORK'S GLOBAL GLADIATORS

In 1955, Chase National Bank merged with the Bank of The Manhattan Company, to create the biggest bank in New York, with an aspiration to be 'the leading commercial banking institution in the world'. Its stunned rival National City Bank (NCB) quickly responded by buying First National Bank, a smaller New York bank. The scene was set for a gladiatorial contest between Chase and Citibank, New York's pioneers of global banking. They were swift to exploit the new Eurocurrency market, which was driven by the Soviet desire to hold dollars offshore to the USA, in order to avoid the risk of confiscation. They had a head start on European and Japanese banks, which were heavily regulated and far from entrepreneurial, whereas their lumbering US peer, Bank of America, grew fat on its vast retail base in California and was slow to seize the global prize.

Dozens of mergers and acquisitions later, Chase and Citibank were the core of two highly diversified financial conglomerates operating in every corner of the globe and riddled with conflicts of interest – a headache for regulator and management alike. In the process, a friendly service to the small man rather got left on one side.

AND...

Political & general

Feb Baghdad Pact against communism between Turkey and Iraq, then UK and Iran (lasted 4 years).

Apr Anthony Eden succeeds Winston Churchill as British premier. Bandung Conference of non-aligned nations, keen to have their own voice in the world.

May End of occupation of West Germany by three World War II victors; East Germany remains Soviet satellite for another 35 years, Austria gains independence. Warsaw Pact signed – military pact between Soviet Union and satellites.

Jun Messina conference to promote European integration; boycotted by UK.

Business & finance

Japan produces 20,000 cars (compare 1980).

Sep First advertisement on UK's commercial TV channel – for Gibbs SR toothpaste; hitherto BBC had a TV monopoly.

Jul Disneyland opened at Anaheim, California.

Dec AFL-CIO merger in USA, forming 16-million-strong labour union.

1956

BRITANNIA RULES THE WAVES

It was a cruel paradox that British Prime Minister Anthony Eden should have joined in the invasion of Egypt, in October 1956, after President Nasser seized the Suez Canal, egged on by Moscow. Eden was, after all, an Arabic scholar. Universal hostility forced a speedy abandonment of this imperial adventure; the last straw was America's failure to support sterling and the freezing of Britain's assets, although this ultimately helped Britain, when Arab (like Soviet) investors, fearful of confiscation, moved their money from New York to London's fast growing Eurocurrency market.

Bankruptcy now stared Britain in the face; a once great nation reminded the German leader, Konrad Adenauer, of a millionaire who did not know that he had lost all his money. Eden, a broken man, resigned and was succeeded by the Chancellor of the Exchequer, Harold Macmillan, who had been a publisher before achieving high office.

It was neither the first nor the last time that Britain would be buffeted by global markets. The Sterling Area, a legacy of empire, brought heavy responsibility, with little reward. Economic and financial crises were to crop up with distressing regularity and it would be another quarter of a century before Britain could shake off the title of 'sick man of Europe'. Britannia ruled the waves no more; at best she might be able to influence them.

AND...

Political & general

Feb Khrushchev denounces Stalin at 20th Party Congress in Moscow; hopes of Soviet reforms.

Jun Because of Egypt's increasingly close ties to Soviet Union, USA cancels aid for Aswan Dam; President Nasser says that he will fund it by nationalizing Suez Canal.

Oct British–French and Israeli invasion of Egypt and subsequent withdrawal under massive international pressure.

Soviet suppression of Hungarian Revolution; Polish rebellion put down by Polish troops.

Nov Khrushchev announces that 'history is on our side; we will bury you' to startled diplomats in Moscow.

Business & finance

Jan Ford Motor Company shares offered to the public for the first time, through Goldman Sachs.

Nov UK loses $279 million of reserves in a single month, through the foreign exchange markets.

'I suppose it would be silly to hope that the Russians might sell the
Egyptians up the river before the Americans sell us?'

'Dear Mr Macmillan, I was so thrilled when they made you Prime
Minister; I've always admired you and I wish you every success.
P.S. I enclose the manuscript of my first novel
for your kind consideration.'

'I got here before "inside dealing" became a crime.'

1957

A NOD AND A WINK

In September 1957, hoping to curb inflation and avert another sterling crisis, the Bank of England lifted its Bank Rate to the unprecedented level of 7%. Some of its directors were accused of using inside information to their financial advantage, but a public inquiry exonerated them. It was the first time that most Brits had heard of insider dealing – a crime hard to track down, as there is usually no paper trail and information often passes by a nod and a wink. It is a blot and a brake on the workings of capitalism, but few offenders are caught and fewer still sent to jail for it.

When the missionaries of Anglo-Saxon capitalism began to preach their message around the globe in the eighties, they usually carried a draft securities law in their briefcases; but what were the chances of putting a Palermo mafioso, a Muscovite oligarch or a sheikh of Araby behind bars for insider dealing?

AND...

Political & general

Jan Eden, his health broken, resigns as British premier and is succeeded by Macmillan.

Mar Treaty of Rome sets up the European Economic Community; initial members France, West Germany, Italy, Netherlands, Belgium and Luxembourg. It signifies first step to 'an even closer union among the European peoples'. Eisenhower and Macmillan meet in Bermuda to restore the Anglo-American 'special relationship', damaged by Suez crisis.

Sep President Eisenhower sends troops to ensure school integration in Little Rock, Arkansas.

Oct USA shocked at Soviet launch of satellite *Sputnik*. Launches programme to catch up, leading to formation of NASA. Dutch expelled from Indonesia.

Business & finance

Mar Sony introduces its first transistor radio.

May Deutsche Bank, having been split into 3 regional units after the war, is reunited under Hermann Abs.

Sep Bank Rate rose to its highest ever level of 7% to protect sterling and restrain inflation. American Motors introduces first compact car in US market, the Rambler, as alternative to 'gas guzzling dinosaurs'. Cult of the equity grows in UK – launch of Unicorn Unit Trust and pioneering equity investment by George Ross-Goobey of Imperial Tobacco Pension Fund, despite City of London scepticism.

'... with this difference, this time the take-over bid will be effected
without any promise that all employees will retain their jobs.'

1958

THE GREAT ALUMINIUM WAR

As the Bank Rate came down from its 7% crisis level, Britain's rising stock market set the scene for the 'Great Aluminium War' in December 1958. Two US companies, ALCOA and Reynolds Metals, slugged it out for control of The British Aluminium Company. It was a bitter and bruising battle, in which the *arriviste* firm of SG Warburg & Co took on the old City of London banking houses and won. The City's style of business would never be the same again; hitherto, mergers and acquisitions were usually conducted with a veneer of good manners, but now it was each man for himself.

Merger and acquisition advice was to be a fertile field for the City's merchant bankers – they owed a lot to Sir Siegmund Warburg, the banker from Hamburg who had imported brutal takeover tactics, red in tooth and claw, from America and shaken up the establishment. The M & A business developed mightily in the UK and then went global. Forty years later, the City's banks and their attendant professional advisors had a big share of the business, though most of them were no longer in British ownership.

AND...

Political & general

May 'Great Leap Forward' driven by Mao Tse-tung; attempt to hasten economic development of China, with disastrous effects on industry and agriculture.
Jun Military revolt in Algeria and Corsica brings Charles de Gaulle out of 12-year retirement to become French premier.
Jul Military coup in Iraq; monarchy overthrown. US marines sent to Lebanon to maintain stability. UK race riots in Notting Hill lead to race relations legislation.
Oct Election of Pope John XXIII. Boris Pasternak, author of *Doctor Zhivago* and winner of Nobel Prize for literature, subject to vitriolic persecution in Soviet Union.
Dec Fidel Castro ousts dictator of Cuba, Fulgencio Batista, and launches Marxist-Leninist Programme.

Business & finance

Publication of *Parkinson's Law*, a satirical book on human organizational behaviour, including the notable quotation: 'Work expands so as to fill the time available for its completion.'
Apr Disastrous diversification by UK drinks company Distillers, which takes on distribution of thalidomide, a drug which turned out to induce birth defects.
Jul Big UK banks take stakes in hire purchase companies, stimulating consumer credit.
Oct First transatlantic passenger jet flights by BOAC and PAN AM.
Dec UK Treasury ministers resign over government expenditure, as Macmillan promotes consumer boom.

'When the music stops, those without seats are declared redundant under the terms of the merger.'

'Nothing wrong with being involved at school in pay awards, token strikes, working to rule. All good stuff for later life ...'

'Officially it's an unofficial strike, but unofficially it's an official one.'

1959

I'M ALL RIGHT, JACK

Ever since William Pitt brought in the Combination Acts of 1799 and 1800, industrial workers have been trying to get organized to better their conditions and pay. The British concept of trade unionism swept the world; even communist countries, where industry was supposedly owned by the workers, had trade unions. But in due course they frequently became an impediment to business growth and, in some cases, were seriously infected by crime.

The 1959 film *I'm All Right Jack*, starring Peter Sellers, was a wicked satire on the British trade unionists. Britain's economy was hamstrung by official and unofficial strikes, go-slows and works-to-rule; the City had no chance of resuming global finance leadership with sterling constantly rocked by inflationary wage demands, both in the nationalized industries and in the private sector. The Tories could never solve the problem, while Labour would settle matters with union leaders over 'beer and sandwiches' at 10 Downing Street. Labour's Barbara Castle produced reform proposals, *In Place of Strife*, in 1969, but she was seen off by union leaders, her party's paymasters.

Margaret Thatcher outlawed the worst practices and broke the power of the unions in the early eighties. Under her premiership, Rupert Murdoch defeated the print unions and moved *The Times* to a new computerized printing plant at Wapping; you either had to admire or hate him for his success. When Tony Blair became prime minister in 1997, beer and sandwiches looked like they might be back on the menu in Downing Street, perhaps with Chardonnay as an alternative, in keeping with his desire to be 'at the heart of Europe'.

AND...

Political & general

Jan de Gaulle inaugurated president of the French Fifth Republic, with greater powers; proposes self-determination for Algeria. Alaska admitted as 49th US state; Hawaii becomes 50th later in same year.
Mar Dalai Lama leaves Tibet, after Chinese intensify occupation; immigrations of many Han Chinese.
Oct After stock market rise and higher consumer expenditure, Conservatives win UK election. Macmillan coined slogan: 'You never had it so good.'

Business & finance

Jun St Lawrence Seaway opened, promoting development of the Great Lakes area.
Jul Hovercraft, an air-cushioned vehicle able to cross water, ice or marsh and invented by Sir Christopher Cockerell, makes first crossing of English Channel.
Nov UK and 6 other nations form European Free Trade Association, for trading co-operation, without political integration. End of 116-day US steel strike.

'And the Lord said, "They shall gradually, so as not to cause
unemployment, beat their swords into ploughshares."'

1960

MERCHANTS OF DEATH

In May 1960 an American pilot, Gary Powers, was taking pictures of Soviet military sites high above Sverdlovsk in the Urals; his U2 spy plane was shot down and he was put on trial in Moscow. 'We caught them as you would a thief with his hand in your pocket,' said the Soviet leader, Nikita Khrushchev. No wonder a four-power summit in Paris, intended to dampen the Cold War and curtail the arms race, broke up in disarray. The veteran Politburo member, Anastas Mikoyan, later said that the U2 affair had delayed détente for 15 years. For the peace-loving old soldier Dwight D Eisenhower it was a sad and humiliating autumn to his presidency, since he had – albeit reluctantly – authorized the fatal flight and was then caught out attempting to deny it.

In his farewell to the nation, Eisenhower gave a strong warning against the influence of the 'military-industrial complex', but it didn't have much effect. American arms sales rose from $300 million to $1.7 billion in the sixties; British and French sales also rose. The Soviet Union rearmed itself, its satellites and its new clients, such as Egypt, South Yemen and Cuba.

It was hard to control the global arms race – apart from the strategic considerations, it yielded profits and jobs at home and helped the balance of payments. Arms selling became a respectable profession; fifty years earlier, you were a merchant of death, now you were a corporate vice-president, with nothing to stop you being a member of the country club. But the arms race certainly kept the Cold War bubbling, while the attendant trade and investment flows contributed significantly to globalization.

AND...

Political & general

Feb UK Premier Macmillan visits South Africa; his words 'The wind of change is blowing over this continent' stressed decolonization and criticized apartheid.
Apr Chinese accusations of 'revisionism' lead to bitter Sino-Soviet schism and withdrawal of thousands of Soviet advisors.
May Adolf Eichmann, former SS officer, kidnapped in Argentina and brought to trial in Israel for crimes against Jews.
Jul Disturbances in Congo as Belgium withdraws as colonial power. Mrs Sirimavo Bandaranaike premier of Sri Lanka – first woman in the world to hold this position.

Business & finance

Sep Organization of Petroleum Exporting Countries (OPEC) formed.
Dec Organization for Economic Co-operation and Development formed by USA, Canada and 18 European nations.

'Dinner was absolutely delicious, and thanks again for the bombers.'

'It's been moved and seconded that we fly the company plane to Zurich,
split the bank accounts, and go our merry ways.'

1961

THE GNOMES OF ZURICH

The Swiss were global bankers *par excellence*; they thrived on the Cold War – just as they had on World War II, when funds streamed into their coffers from belligerents, neutrals, persecutors and persecuted. To British Prime Minister Harold Wilson, they were the 'gnomes of Zurich' – faceless bankers whose sales of sterling could knock the British economy off course. With their system of numbered accounts, secrecy, and freedom from tax and exchange controls, they attracted a lot of money in troubled times, such as August 1961 when the Berlin Wall was built to keep the two Germanys apart.

The Swiss banks were often suspected of harbouring dirty money, from third world dictators, common criminals or simple tax evaders. From the eighties they began to freeze and return funds looted from countries such as the Philippines and Nigeria; they also clamped down on terrorists and other criminals using Swiss banks. But, to the fury of its neighbours, Switzerland continues to turn a blind eye to evasion of other countries' taxes and insider-dealing laws. So it's not surprising that, at the end of the twentieth century, Swiss banks were thought to be managing over a quarter of the world's individual wealth held offshore and that two of their banks were among the global top twenty.

AND...

Political & general

Jan John Kennedy President, Lyndon Johnson Vice President of the USA.
Feb Britain and Iceland settle bitter dispute over fishing: 'Cod War' (resumes 1972). Kuwait independent; immediate challenge by Iraq, rebuffed with British aid.
Apr Failed invasion of Cuba by Cuban exiles, run by CIA ('Bay of Pigs'). First man in orbit, Yuri Gagarin of Soviet Union. French military revolt in Algiers in protest at prospect of Algerian independence, rapidly quelled by de Gaulle.
Sep UN Secretary General Dag Hammarskjöld killed in Congo peace mission.

Business & finance

Citibank introduces Certificates of Deposit in New York.
Jul Lord Cromer succeeds Lord Cobbold as Bank of England Governor – at 42, the youngest to hold the post since the 18th century.
Dec Imperial Chemical Industries is thwarted in its attempt to buy textile group Courtaulds. At that time represents largest UK corporate takeover bid.

'Good morning, sir! I represent Rupert Murdoch.
We bought a controlling interest in you as you slept.'

1962

WOLLONGONG TODAY, TOMORROW THE WORLD

The July 1962 launch into orbit of TELSTAR marked the birth of satellite broadcasting. Weeks later, hearings began over who should be awarded a Sydney television licence; Rupert Murdoch, a young newspaperman from Adelaide, thought that he had it in the bag, but he was 'in too much of a hurry' for the monarchical Australian Prime Minister Sir Robert Menzies. Instead, he had a piece of the Wollongong licence, just outside Sydney, but within viewing range; he then acquired 2,500 hours of popular US programming and gave the people what they wanted – to his great profit. It was an early example of the chutzpah that would propel Murdoch's News Corporation to global leadership in books, newspapers, films and television.

Murdoch bestowed his political blessings erratically; he backed and then ditched Australia's Labour Prime Minister Gough Whitlam, and he supported both Carter and Reagan. After his UK tabloid the *Sun* suddenly decided to back the Tories in the 1992 election, its headline said it all: 'IT'S THE SUN WOT WON IT'. Murdoch's political influence was transient but the awesome reach of satellite broadcasting was there for good. Could traditional societies survive the onslaught of new ideas and temptations? Could the world's linguistic diversity survive the pervasive intrusion of the English language? How could governments control or tax the broadcasters? One country gave it a try; President Jiang Ze-min wanted to restrict information 'not conducive to China's development'. The Great Wall had separated foreigners and Chinese for many centuries: could an electronic wall do the same?

AND...

Political & general

Jan Common Agricultural Policy launched; large subsidies to European Economic Community farmers, regularly modified over the ensuing decades.

Feb Colonel John Glenn (later US Senator) launched into orbit to be first US astronaut.

Jul Declaration of independence of Algeria, after referenda. 'Night of the Long Knives' – UK Premier Macmillan sacks 7 ministers. President Kennedy's 'Grand Design' for European-American co-operation rejected by President de Gaulle.

Oct Kennedy outfaces Khrushchev in Cuban missile crisis.

Business & finance

Warren Buffett buys into ailing New England textile company, Berkshire Hathaway, which he steers into highly successful diversification.

Apr President Kennedy insists that US steel companies rescind price rises.

May 'Black Monday' – Dow Jones Index falls a record 5.7% on fears of a recession, followed by 6.4% fall in London the next day.

Jul First Wal-Mart store opens at Rogers, Arkansas.

'Today, in a surprise move, everyone in the media
veered slightly to the right.'

'Bank of England ... Inquiries? As a matter of interest,
I should like to know whether Mr O'Brien, the new Chief Cashier,
spells his name with an apostrophe.'

1963

ROBBING THE BANK

Banks suffered from two particularly striking crimes in 1963. An armed gang held up a train on its way from Scotland to London and stole £2.5 million in used banknotes, and in the same year it emerged that Allied Crude Vegetable Oil Refining had raised $175 million from banks mainly on the security of sea water instead of the pure salad oil it was claimed to be. The fraud rocked American Express Company, whose tanks in New Jersey stored the security, and sent its perpetrator, the so-called 'salad oil king', Tino de Angelis, to jail for seven years.

The Eurocurrency market was taking root; it was no longer just a haven for Soviet and Arab deposits and was set to grow explosively from $12 billion to $5 trillion over the next 25 years. European banks, shackled to their cosy and regulated business at home, took to the new global business with gusto; just because the US dollar was master of the world, did this mean the American banks should skim off the cream of the business? But managing new activities, unfamiliar customers and distant outposts proved difficult; banks made far larger losses from fraud, bad lending, derivatives and foreign exchange than they ever lost to robbers or forgers.

AND...

Political & general

Jan de Gaulle blocks UK entry into European Economic Community; launches Franco-German Treaty of Friendship as route to French hegemony in Europe.
May Organization of African Unity formed, after widespread decolonization.
Jun President Kennedy visits Berlin and inspires its citizens by declaring 'Ich bin ein Berliner.' Election of Pope Paul VI.
Jun Profumo scandal in UK. Equal Pay Act in USA.
Aug Nuclear Test Ban Treaty. 200,000 in Washington on civil rights march; Rev. Martin Luther King 'I have a dream...'.
Oct Douglas-Home succeeds Macmillan as UK premier. Erhard succeeds Adenauer as German Chancellor.
Nov President Kennedy assassinated, succeeded by Johnson.

Business & finance

May 'Kennedy Round' – Geneva negotiations to reduce international tariffs under The General Agreement on Tariffs and Trade (GATT).
Jul US Interest Equalization Tax stems US capital outflows, international bond market gravitates from New York to London, SG Warburg & Co issues first Eurobond – for Italian motorways company, Autostrade.
Dec US car-makers reduced to 4 (there were 44 in 1925), as Studebaker ceases production. First US nuclear power station at Oyster Creek, New Jersey.

1964

AFTER A GOOD LUNCH

Although US exports comfortably exceeded imports, the American Treasury Secretary, Douglas Dillon, fretted at the capital outflows from foreign borrowings in New York and US investments abroad. So controls and taxes were introduced, which boosted the Eurocurrency market. It was a fabulous opportunity for the City of London; new financing techniques were invented, such as the Eurobond and the Euroloan, and new types of institution were created to do what the staid old domestic banks could not or would not do.

One such institution was the consortium bank, or Eurobank, an entity owned by other banks to do Eurocurrency business. The first was born in 1964 and was followed by 34 others. Every self-respecting bank had to be in on the act, as it seemed to be a shortcut to profiting from the fast growing Euroloan market. Ad hoc groups of banks from different countries joined forces to set up Eurobanks, often with little forethought – Orion Bank's David Montagu scornfully said that some were 'formed after a good lunch'.

Soon the Eurobanks were competing with their owners, which naturally kept the best business for themselves. They scoured the world for new clients and, in the process, made many bad loans to developing countries. Most of these banks had gone out of business by 1990 but they made an important contribution to the globalization of the banking business.

AND...

Political & general

Jan US Surgeon General links smoking and cancer, confirming what England's James I said over 300 years ago: 'tobacco is dangerous to the lungs'. Palestine Liberation Organization (PLO) established.
May Intensified personality cult in China; 350 million copies of *Quotations of Chairman Mao* printed in next four years.
Jun Mandela jailed for opposing apartheid in South Africa.
Jul US Civil Rights Act.
Aug Tonkin Gulf incident raises US Vietnam commitment.
Oct Harold Wilson, Labour, elected UK premier. Nikita Khrushchev replaced by Leonid Brezhnev as Soviet leader. China drops its first atomic bomb.

Business & finance

Mar German 25% coupon tax on domestic issues stimulates DM Eurobond market.
Apr IBM introduces 360 Series of compatible computers – ensuring continued leadership in the sector. Also produces the Magnetic Tape Selective Typewriter, forerunner of the word processor. Ford's Mustang launched – first popular sports car in USA.
Oct Concerted help is given by G10 countries to protect sterling.

'The way they toss their funds around, they're heading for default!'

'We might make unwise international loans, Mr Simpson,
but we don't make unwise loans to individuals.'

'Fortunately, you have the life savings of a man three times your age.'

1965

PAYING THE DOCTOR

When Britain's National Health Service was set up in 1948, it was to be free for all 'at the point of delivery', but managerial and financial problems have frustrated this noble aim; it now co-habits uneasily with a growing private sector. For the ill and old of the USA, the passing of the Medicare bill in 1965 was a great boon, but the cost of medical services continued to bear hard on many Americans.

The insatiable desire for better health, the increasing average age of people and advances in technology have been good for the suppliers of pharmaceuticals and medical equipment; at the end of the century, three of them were numbered among the ten most profitable global companies, each earning more than 20% on revenues. If you were prescient or lucky enough to have invested £1,000 in a small UK company, Glaxo Laboratories, when it came to market in 1947, and hung on to your stake through merger after merger, you would have had shares in GlaxoSmithKline worth £500,000.

Globalization protestors often targeted drug companies for the apparently high price of medicines, but how could new drugs be developed without profits to pay for research, much of which was likely to prove abortive?

AND...

Political & general

Jan Death of Sir Winston Churchill. President Johnson pledges 'Great Society' for America.
Mar Nicolae Ceausescu becomes leader of Romania; develops policy of independence from Soviet Union.
Jun Army takes power in Algeria.
Aug Singapore secures independence from Malaysia and becomes a major trading and financial centre.
Nov Unilateral Declaration of Independence by Rhodesia; sanctions and 15 years of instability. Sese Seko Mobutu takes power in Congo (Zaire).
Dec Ferdinand Marcos Philippine president.

Business & finance

Feb President de Gaulle attacks dollar hegemony and gold/dollar exchange rate of $35 an ounce; French reserves switched into gold. US Voluntary Foreign Credit Restraint Program; US corporates tap Eurobond market.
Nov Ralph Nader's *Unsafe at Any Speed* leads to car safety legislation and increased manufacturing costs.
Dec Asian Development Bank formed, to supplement World Bank activity in Asia.

'But, General, if we do let the world's banking system collapse, bang goes everything we've managed to salt away abroad.'

1966

OUR SON OF A BITCH

Dictatorships were cropping up everywhere. In 1966 Suharto began his long reign in Indonesia, joining three other members of the durable dictators club, Mobutu of Congo, Boumedienne of Algeria and Marcos of the Philippines, who had all seized power the year before. America was being sucked ever more deeply into the morass of Vietnam and dictators helped stem the global spread of communism. The typical dictator was a military man, often incompetent, nasty and corrupt – in CIA parlance, 'a son of a bitch, but at least he's our son of a bitch'.

Once in power, the dictators and their families could amass great wealth and satisfy their wildest whims, from collecting 3,000 pairs of shoes (Imelda Marcos) to being crowned emperor (Jean-Bedel Bokassa). However, arms expenditure left many poor countries heavily indebted with little to show for it; much of the money was salted away in Swiss banks or offshore units of the very banks that had lent it. When Argentina embarked on its Falklands adventure, its citizens were estimated to be holding $40 billion of assets abroad. Was it coincidence that this just happened to equate to its international debts?

In due course, the fresh winds of economic globalization would blow away most of the dictators. Democracy, often flawed, took their place.

AND...

Political & general

Jan Indira Gandhi, daughter of Pandit Nehru, becomes Indian premier.
Feb Soviet-Cuban trade agreement ties Cuba to Moscow.
Mar General Suharto takes power from President Sukarno in Indonesia; bloody purge of communists.
Apr America first uses B-52 bombers against North Vietnam.
Aug Cultural Revolution in China strengthens Mao Tse-tung; young Red Guards set out to purify communism; Deng Xiao-ping and other leaders disgraced for 'taking the capitalist road'.
Sep President Hendrik Verwoerd, architect of apartheid in South Africa, assassinated.
Nov Erhard replaced as German Chancellor by Kurt Kiesinger.

Business & finance

May UK economy 'blown off course' by seamen's strike. Citibank issues negotiable Eurodollar CDs in London. Fiat builds car plant in Soviet Union – US worries about plant helping North Vietnam, now receiving increased Soviet support.
Jul Leslie O'Brien succeeds Lord Cromer as Bank of England Governor; first appointment of an 'insider' in modern times.
Nov Bank of America licenses other banks to use its credit card; rise of VISA and Master Charge.

'And so, in the sunset of my life, I am resigning the Party chairmanship,
the Premiership, and the Presidency. God bless you all.
I will, of course, continue as Head of State.'

'I suspect you of driving under the influence of America.'

'And France thinks "special provisional probationary transitional associate membership" is still a little too positive.'

1967

NON, NON, MONSIEUR WILSON

'Durham miners won't wear it,' said Labour minister Herbert Morrison, while Tory minister RA Butler dismissed as 'archaeological excavations' a meeting in Messina to plan European unity. So it was hardly surprising when, in 1967, for the second time, France vetoed Britain's application to join the European Economic Community. President de Gaulle told Prime Minister Harold Wilson that the British needed 'a profound economic and political transformation which could allow them to join the Six Continentals'. He mistrusted Britain's 'special relationship' with America, its Commonwealth links and its aspirations to global leadership in finance. He was in a touchy mood, having just been turfed out of Canada by his hosts for proclaiming 'Vive le Québec libre' from the balcony of Montreal's Hôtel de Ville.

Dictatorships had ruined Europe in the thirties and forties; two still survived from that era in Portugal and Spain, when Greece was suddenly taken over by a cabal of colonels. Everywhere there was a great aspiration for peace, prosperity and democracy. Could it best come through 'ever closer union of the peoples of Europe', as envisaged in the Treaty of Rome? Or through the free movement of trade, investment and peoples, without undoing the existing states, as preferred by Britain and Scandinavia? This was the dilemma that was to divide Europe for 50 years, if not more.

AND...

Political & general

Mar Moscow horrified as Stalin's favourite child, Svetlana, seeks US asylum.

Apr Colonels take power in Greece.

May Secession of Biafra; civil war in Nigeria (to 1970).

Jun Six-Day War in the Middle East; brief oil embargo; Palestinians flee to Jordan.

Nov United Nations declaration on equality of women. Former British colony becomes Soviet satellite, People's Democratic Republic of Yemen.

Dec Dr Christiaan Barnard performs first heart transplant in Cape Town.

Business & finance

Mar *Torrey Canyon* spills 120,000 tons of oil off England. Atlantic Richfield finds 10 billion barrel oil field in Alaska (largest in North America).

Apr US aircraft manufacturers merge; Douglas and McDonnell.

Jul Launch of European Airbus consortium.

Nov The pound is devalued from $2.80 to $2.40, after record balance of payments deficit. Britain's General Electric Company acquires AEI (adding English Electric in 1968), to create largest UK manufacturing group.

Dec Milton Friedman urges floating exchange rates and freedom to trade foreign currencies. Muriel Siebert first woman member of New York Stock Exchange.

'If you can't trust one of Nader's Raiders, who can you trust?'

1968

UNSAFE AT ANY SPEED

To Campbell Soup president William Murphy it was a fad '...of the same order as the hula hoop', but Ralph Nader's car safety campaign was to have a longer shelf life than any tomato soup. His book *Unsafe at Any Speed* transformed the way cars were made everywhere. In June 1968 he formed his first little band of crusaders, 'Nader's Raiders', and tackled abuse after abuse. Nader was one of a motley body of global protestors, from individual anarchists to multinational organizations, which tapped into anxieties about environmental issues, governmental arrogance, corporate misbehaviour and globalization's amorphous threat. Even in Brezhnev's Siberia, 'informals' could halt the pollution of Lake Baikal's crystalline waters.

It was a year of immense political protest. Martin Luther King's assassination by a white assailant provoked widespread riots; anti-war demonstrators were brutally suppressed in Chicago, as American troops in Vietnam rose to over 500,000. French students and workers brought the country to a halt; in Prague, no amount of protest could save 'Socialism with a Human Face' from the Soviet army's ruthless attentions.

Consumerism has had a picturesque history since the citizens of Nottingham rolled huge cheeses down the streets in 1764 and flattened the mayor, in protest at price rises. Nader brought discipline to a wild and woolly movement; he brought protest into the mainstream and could even aspire to the presidency. Nobody could now ignore Nader's Raiders and their ilk.

AND...

Political & general

Apr Pierre Trudeau Canadian premier. Enoch Powell 'Rivers of Blood' speech on UK immigration.

May Riots and strikes (*événements de mai*) threaten French government, but Gaullists do well in subsequent elections.

Jun Tet offensive is set back for USA in Vietnam; violent anti-war protests across USA. Senator Robert Kennedy assassinated.

Jul Nuclear Non-proliferation Treaty. Ba'athists take power in Iraq – rise of Saddam Hussein.

Aug Soviet Union, with other Warsaw Pact countries, suppresses 'Prague Spring' reforms in Czechoslovakia.

Business & finance

Jan US Mandatory Foreign Investment Program. British Leyland Motor Corp set up – forlorn aim to rationalize UK vehicle industry.

Mar Loss of confidence in currencies creates gold rush; official gold pool replaced by dual market.

Aug Largest tanker, 312,000-ton *Universe Ireland*, brings economies of size, but environmental worries.

Nov Large capital inflows into Germany; de Gaulle calls plan to devalue the franc 'worst form of absurdity' but next year his successor, President Pompidou, did exactly that.

'What do we do about flushing the toilet?'

'These projected figures are a figment of our imagination.
We hope you like them.'

'Melville's an economist. In his predictions he's been right just once in a hundred, enough to give him a considerable reputation.'

1969

THE DISMAL SCIENCE

Far from the global turmoil, in Stockholm in 1969, the first Nobel Prize was awarded for economics – Thomas Carlyle's 'dismal science'. It came too late for Maynard Keynes, who had died in 1946, worn out by his efforts to establish a durable postwar financial order.

An early winner was Milton Friedman, eloquent advocate of free markets. When he helped the Chicago Mercantile Exchange introduce financial derivatives, the Chicago traders were dismissed as a 'bunch of crap shooters in pork bellies'; 30 years later it was a $100 trillion global business. When General Pinochet seized power in Chile, Friedman's pupils, the 'Chicago boys', made it the economic star of the South. Friedman said that Chile's economic reforms needed democracy, and democracy was duly restored. Rejected by the electorate, Pinochet looked set to die in his bed, reviled or revered, according to your point of view.

Economists were often hired to forecast the future but their forecasts could be derailed by the irrationality of man or the vagaries of nature. Years later, when two Nobel laureates teamed up to advise an ambitious hedge fund, LTCM, it made immense losses and the world's financial system narrowly averted meltdown. Mesmerized by the grandeur and complexity of their deals, LTCM had not sufficiently allowed for Russia defaulting and devaluing; it did not help the reputation of economists.

AND...

Political & general

Jan Richard Nixon president of the USA.
Feb Yasser Arafat elected Chairman of PLO.
Mar Death of Eisenhower. Clashes on Sino-Soviet border.
Apr de Gaulle resigns as President of France; *Jun* succeeded by Georges Pompidou.
Jul Juan Carlos nominated future King by Francisco Franco, Spanish head of state. Apollo II lands two men on the moon.
Sep Ho Chi Minh dies. Muammar Gaddafi takes power in Libya.
Oct Willy Brandt succeeds Kurt Kiesinger as German Chancellor. Huge peaceful anti-war demonstrations in USA.
Nov US-Soviet arms limitation talks (SALT).

Business & finance

Jan Rupert Murdoch buys *News of the World* – his first big move outside Australia.
Feb AIBD (later International Securities Market Association) formed to improve Eurobond market dealing procedures.
Mar Maiden flight of Concorde, supersonic airliner.
Jun IMF launches Special Drawing Rights to increase international reserves.
Euromoney magazine started.
Sep Bernie Cornfeld floats Investors Overseas Services (he would ask employees 'do you sincerely want to be rich?') – heavy losses befell investors in 1970 when IOS was acquired and looted by ICC.

'What's the delay this morning –
still waiting for a relief NUR general-secretary?'

1970

THE WRONG SORT OF SNOW

As global convergence gathered pace, one industry seemed stuck in its national rut. Railroad companies were the lynchpin of equity markets and prime instruments of globalization in the 1800s; often financed from the City of London, they built America, but a century later they had fallen on evil times. It was hard to meet demands for cheap, regular, uncrowded and safe public transport, as people switched to cars, buses or aircraft. Penn Central and other US railroad companies went under in 1970 and passenger services were assured by the federally supported company, AMTRAK; but it was hand-to-mouth finance and might disappear at any time.

British Rail, nationalized inheritor of 130 predecessor railway companies, had its own problems, often being crippled by the demands of its unions, NUR and ASLEF – acronyms engraved on every commuter's heart. BR's excuses for delays and cancellations ('The wrong sort of snow' or 'Leaves on the line') are the stuff of legend. When BR was privatized in 1996 there was a whiff of global excitement, as companies from France and Wisconsin joined the party, but they would find it hard to prosper under Britain's complex and intrusive regulatory framework.

Once the hottest of all, railway shares were now stock market Cinderellas; perhaps today's high-tech shares would join them one day.

AND...

Political & general

Jan End of Nigerian civil war.
Apr US incursion into Cambodia.
May Violent protests at Kent State University, Ohio, over Vietnam.
Jun Conservatives win election in UK; Edward Heath premier.
Jul Environmental Protection Agency set up in USA.
Sep Palestinian hijacking of planes, crisis in Jordan ('Black September'), expulsion of Palestinian fighters. Salvador Allende wins election in Chile and (despite US attempts to stop him) becomes president; launches Marxist programme. Anwar Sadat president of Egypt after Nasser's death.
Nov Death of de Gaulle. Hafez Assad takes power in Syria.

Business & finance

Jan First transatlantic flight by jumbo jet, Boeing 747.
Mar Richard Branson (aged 20) starts Virgin Group. Pirelli and Dunlop attempt cross-border tyre merger; it failed.
May Werner Report points the way to EEC economic and monetary union.
Sep Libya squeezes tough terms out of Occidental Petroleum; the big oil companies have to follow suit. Similar strategies from other OPEC producers.
Oct Consortium bank, Orion, formed by six of the largest multinational banks to exploit Euromarkets.

'When the roll is called up yonder, I shall be very much surprised if any of the Penn Central management people are there.'

*'I've called the family together to announce that, because of inflation,
I'm going to have to let two of you go.'*

STEVENSON

'OK. *The forward rate for marks rose in March and April, combined with a sharp increase in German reserves and heavy borrowing in the Eurodollar market, while the United States liquid reserves had dropped to fourteen billion dollars, causing speculation that the mark might rise and encouraging conversion on a large scale.*
Now *do you understand?'*

1971

ANXIOUS AMERICANS

It was an anxious time for Americans. The nation was heading for its first trade deficit in living memory, inflation was over 5% and the Vietnam War was stubbornly unfinished. In August 1971 President Nixon introduced some odd measures for a Republican president – import taxes, wage and price controls and suspension of the dollar's convertibility into gold. Then, the dollar was humiliatingly devalued against the currencies of Germany and Japan.

Halfway around the globe, the oil producers were feeling their oats. From his peacock throne, the Shah invited the world to a $100-million bash at Persepolis to celebrate 2,500 years of Persian monarchy; the new kid on the block in Libya, Muammar Gaddafi, successfully played Armand Hammer's Occidental Petroleum off against the oil majors; the young Saddam Hussein plotted to nationalize Iraq's oil, with Soviet support and French connivance; and the emollient Saudi oil minister, Sheikh Ahmed Zaki Yamani, was making friends all round. But the message was the same: we want a bigger slice of the cake, we want it now and we want more dollars to make up for their lost value. Add to OPEC's gripe the Arab–Israeli feud and here were all the ingredients for big trouble; the first 'oil shock' was waiting around the corner to knock the global economy off course.

America's mild anxiety would soon become a throbbing headache.

AND...

Political & general

Formation of Greenpeace – to protest US nuclear test in Aleutian Islands.
Jan Aswan High Dam completed with Soviet help. Idi Amin takes power in Uganda.
Feb Confrontation in Tehran; OPEC extracts concessions from oil companies.
Jul United Arab Emirates proclaimed; Qatar and Bahrain soon get independence, as British withdraw from the Gulf.
Aug Industrial Relations Bill in UK brings contractual frame to labour relations.
Oct China replaces Taiwan at UNO.
Dec Secession of East Pakistan; creation of Bangladesh. Zulfikar Ali Bhutto president of Pakistan.

Business & finance

Feb NASDAQ set up for trading smaller and technology company shares. Decimalization of currency in UK; price rises from 'rounding up'.
Sep New UK 'Competition and Credit Control' policy stimulates inflation and leads to imprudent lending by banks.
Dec G-10 countries meet at Smithsonian Institution, Washington, and repeg exchange rates (US dollar devalued 8% generally, 17% against yen). Gold price rises from $35 to $38, after suspension of dollar convertibility.

'I'm as aware of the evils of communism as anyone, but good God, when you think of eight hundred million Chinese in terms of franchises …'

1972

NIXON GOES A-CALLING

It was a stunning volte-face for President Nixon, scourge of American communists, to call on Mao Tse-tung in February 1972, at the instigation of Henry Kissinger. China was hostile and xenophobic, its political philosophy directly opposed to that of America. Yet the business potential was huge, despite a long history of Chinese self-sufficiency and disdain for all things foreign. Old China hands recalled the fate, in bygone times, of the Robinson Piano Company which reckoned on there being 200 million potential lady pianists in China; quantities of pianos were sent out, but most of them crumbled away in Shanghai and Hong Kong warehouses. Nixon had sown the seed for China's cautious moves, after Mao's death four years later, towards free markets and greater engagement with the global economy. China even began to make pianos.

Next stop Moscow, where Nixon signed an arms limitation agreement with Brezhnev. Perhaps Soviet energy resources could reduce America's increasing dependence on the volatile Middle East? Détente through trade looked like a promising development and Armand Hammer was the man to give it a try; he was well regarded in Moscow, having built a pencil factory for Lenin half a century previously, under the New Economic Policy. But his $20 billion of Soviet projects were stymied by a new surge in the Cold War.

Soon after Nixon came home from these trips, the Watergate break-in took place; his presidency was doomed, despite the grandeur of his global vision.

AND...

Political & general	Business & finance
Jan Strikes, power cuts and inflation in UK; state of emergency declared. 'Bloody Sunday' in Northern Ireland leads to direct British rule.	*Mar* 'Snake' established to stabilize European exchange rates.
Jul Sadat expels 20,000 Soviet advisors from Egypt.	*May* Currency futures contracts introduced by Chicago Mercantile Exchange.
Aug President Amin of Uganda launches mass expulsion of British Asians; many come to UK and prosper there.	*Jun* Under severe pressure, the pound leaves the 'snake'.
Sep Palestinians kill 11 Israeli athletes at Munich Olympics. Start of a second 'Cod War' (earlier one 1961) over fishing rights between UK, Germany and Iceland (to 1976).	*Jul* Negative interest rate on non-resident SF deposits.
	Sep First pocket calculators from Texas Instruments.
	Oct ARPANET launched, precursor of the internet.
	Nov Dow Jones Industrial Average over 1,000 for the first time.

'Look, Nixon's no dope. If the people really wanted moral leadership, he'd give them moral leadership.'

THE SHEIKHS SHAKE THINGS UP, 1973–86

There was never a month quite like October 1973. The Americans were pulling out of Vietnam, US–Soviet détente was settling down and China was being brought in from the cold, when suddenly vicious Arab–Israeli rivalry broke out into war. It happened when the Gulf producers – and the rest of OPEC – were feeling particularly aggrieved about low oil prices. The ensuing price rises pitchforked the world into the worst recession in recent memory.

But global recession did not halt globalization's march – far from it. Rich and poor countries alike needed more money for their pricier oil imports, so international lending, fuelled by petrodollars, quintupled in two years and surged on until it all ended in tears with a huge debt crisis. Trade, after a setback, grew rapidly, as did foreign investment. International securities, foreign exchange and derivatives dealings were spurred by deregulation and technology. Adventurous Arab investors were pioneers of the 'emerging markets', though placing most of their funds in the West. Globalization's momentum was not halted by a Cold War throwback; the Soviets invaded Afghanistan but it proved to be a nail in the coffin of what President Reagan, in an address to Britain's House of Commons, called 'the evil empire'.

After the Arabs came the Japanese as global investors; Japan coped supremely well with the energy crisis and built up an enormous trade surplus, enabling it to make spectacular investments around the globe and to enjoy a brief moment of financial hegemony.

Powerful leaders shaped the era. Margaret Thatcher abolished exchange controls and privatized government companies; her Falklands War, perhaps inadvertently, helped spread democracy in Latin America. Deng Xiao-ping transformed Mao's legacy in China, to make it an industrial giant. The election of a Polish pope and the rise to power of Mikhail Gorbachev undermined the Soviet empire (though this was far from Gorbachev's intention). These leaders created the conditions that would spread Anglo-Saxon capitalism across vast areas of the world.

'By the way, Professor, whatever happened to all that lovely nuclear
power that was going to revolutionize our lives the last time we met?'

'As Adam Smith so aptly put it ...'

'Daddy has simply borrowed your bicycle lamp
to read his evening paper.'

1973

THE LIGHTS GO OUT

The price of oil, virtually unchanged throughout the 1960s, was expressed in US dollars and, when the dollar lost value, the income of the oil-producing countries was seriously hit. In October 1973 the 'Yom Kippur' war broke out between Israel and the Arab states. The oil producers made up for lost time by quadrupling the price of oil and imposing a selective embargo. It was the first 'oil shock'; the lights went out all over Europe and a worldwide recession soon followed.

The income of oil-producing countries rose from $37 billion to $270 billion over seven years. For populous countries, such as Nigeria and Indonesia, the money could be used at home, if it had not been looted by their rulers. For Gulf countries with small populations there were huge surpluses; a new breed of Arab financiers soon learnt how to deploy these surpluses, developing great skill in fending off the endless flow of carpet-baggers that came after their custom. Usually they operated discreetly, but sometimes they made a big splash, as when some Saudi princes teamed up with the Hunts to corner silver in 1980 or when Kuwait tried opportunistically to acquire control of BP during the 1987 stock market crash.

AND...

Political & general

Jan Nixon starts second term as US President; Paris agreement to end Vietnam War. Global fuel shortages and price rises. UK, Denmark and Ireland join EEC.
Jun Brezhnev visits USA and prematurely declares Cold War over. OPEC threatens use of the 'oil weapon'.
Sep General Augusto Pinochet seizes power in Chile; Allende's Marxist policies reversed; 'Chicago boys' introduce market economy.
Oct Yom Kippur war between Arab states and Israel leads to first 'oil shock'. Resignation of US Vice President Agnew over scandal, replaced by Gerald Ford.

Business & finance

Big increase in lending to third world countries – seeds of the future debt crisis.
Feb 10% devaluation of US dollar; other currencies float. First woman member of the London Stock Exchange.
Mar Iran nationalizes foreign oil companies; other OPEC countries pursue same ends less abruptly.
Apr Equity Funding Corp of America charged with fraud. FedEx set up to compete with US Postal Service.
Jul Gordon Richardson succeeds Leslie O'Brien as Bank of England Governor.
Nov Secondary bank crisis; Bank of England 'lifeboat' helps banks hit by bad property and shipping loans.

'For heaven's sake, Alison, you can't leave me before the end of the current tax year. You're deductible.'

1974

ONLY LITTLE PEOPLE PAY TAXES

On top of the 'oil shock', the Tories had to cope with strikes, power cuts and, as usual, a wobbly currency; for Britain, it was the 'gravest situation since the end of the war', said the Chancellor of the Exchequer Anthony Barber. In February 1974 they went to the country and asked the electorate: 'Who governs Britain?' The answer was not Edward Heath's government. Labour was narrowly restored to power and Harold Wilson again took up residence at 10 Downing Street.

But Labour was no more successful at solving Britain's problems than its predecessors. Their solution included more government intervention and higher taxes; Denis Healey, the new Chancellor of the Exchequer, reportedly said that he would 'squeeze the rich until the pips squeaked'. When he raised the top rate of tax to 83% and added a 15% tax on investment income, the rich were indeed squeezed, but they had their deductions and shelters – so the burden fell mainly on middle income people and on business. High taxes went out of fashion in the Thatcher/Reagan era; it became clear that lower taxes stimulated the economy and, paradoxically, increased government revenues. Moreover, globalization made it ever more difficult for governments to get their paws on the money as it whizzed around the world beyond their control.

AND...

Political & general

Jan US Secretary of State Henry Kissinger brokers ceasefire between Egypt and Israel.
Apr President Pompidou of France dies, succeeded by Valéry Giscard d'Estaing. Military coup in Portugal.
May Helmut Schmidt succeeds Willy Brandt as West German Chancellor.
Jul Turks invade Cyprus, leading to partition. Civilian rule restored in Greece.
Aug Watergate scandal forces resignation of President Nixon, succeeded by Vice President Ford.
Sep After 58-year reign, Haile Selassie (the 'Lion of Judah') deposed in Ethiopia by a Marxist junta.

Business & finance

Petrodollar recycling and increased IMF facilities mitigate global recession and inflation. Growing use of word processors as higher energy prices stimulate the search for cost savings in the workplace.
Jan US capital controls abolished.
Feb Dreyfus launches first public money market fund.
May Collapse of Franklin National Bank, 20th largest US bank, headed by fraudster Michele Sindona.
Jun Foreign exchange losses bring down West German bank ID Herstatt and damage several leading banks.
Jul Iran buys 25% of Krupp Steel Corp.
Oct AGEFI financial magazine launched (later *IFR*).

'I suppose one could say it favours the rich, but, on the other hand, it's a great incentive for everyone to make two hundred grand a year.'

'Go home, I tell you! The recession is over!'

'We've tried sun, surf and sand.
Do you have anything in the way of darkness, dankness and despair?'

'All we're asking for are price increases indexed to the rate of inflation caused by increases in oil prices.'

'Look at it this way, Mr Helfrick – the sun is shining, the birds are singing, the bees are humming, inflation is spiralling and the flowers are blooming. Four out of five isn't bad.'

1975

EVERY CLOUD HAS A SILVER LINING

The first 'oil shock' brought on global worry and despair for rich and poor countries alike. 1975 was the second year of a lethal combination of recession and inflation, but the oil embargo did not last long and countries learned to adjust to higher energy costs. OPEC surpluses were recycled to a wide range of countries; Middle East financiers were readier to invest in or lend to third world countries than their Western counterparts and their activities paved the way for the subsequent rise of global emerging markets. The Cold War was going through a period of comparative calm – the Helsinki Accords on détente, signed in August by 35 countries, including the USA and the Soviet Union, seemed a hopeful sign.

Stock markets began to anticipate better times. London's All Share Index, having suffered a dreadful fall of 70% over two and a half years, more than doubled in 1975 to bring some cheer to British investors, despite Labour's higher taxes. In New York the Dow Jones Industrials, which had not fallen so dramatically, rose 40% in a year. But inflation was still over 10% and much of the global economy remained in the doldrums.

AND...

Political & general

Feb Margaret Thatcher replaces Edward Heath as Conservative leader in UK.
Mar King Faisal of Saudi Arabia killed by deranged nephew.
Apr Fall of Saigon leads to reunification of Vietnam under communist rule. Khmer Rouge begins reign of terror in Cambodia. Lebanon's 15-year civil war begins.
Aug Cuba pours advisors into Angola, with much Soviet help, to establish pro-Soviet regime in newly independent nation.
Oct Soviet scientist and human rights campaigner Dr Andrei Sakharov awarded Nobel Peace Prize.
Nov Death of Francisco Franco; Juan Carlos King of Spain.
Dec Indonesia invades East Timor.

Business & finance

Apr Microsoft founded by Bill Gates (aged 19) and Paul Allen (22) to develop microcomputer operating systems.
May Deregulation of US stock market leads to consolidation in US securities firms.
Jun UK commences North Sea oil production.
Aug Co-operation between central banks over cross-border supervision of banks (Basle Concordat).
Sep France agrees to sell nuclear reactor to Iraq 'for peaceful purposes' (Chirac) or as 'first concrete step towards the Arab atomic bomb' (Saddam Hussein).
Nov New York City financing crisis weakens US dollar.

'You're right! It is eating ants!'

1976

ACROSS THE ATLANTIC IN THREE HOURS

It was excellent news amidst the general gloom when the Anglo-French supersonic airliner, Concorde, could finally carry passengers across the Atlantic in April 1976. The transatlantic journey took little more than three hours, compared to Christopher Columbus's 37 days in 1492. Globalization was built on technical innovations in transport; better sails, masts, hulls and rudders in the 15th century enabled the Spanish and Portuguese explorers to cross the oceans and come home to tell the tale. The 18th-century steam engine was an invention comparable to the wheel; it made possible the railways that transformed the world. The 20th-century subsonic and supersonic airliners were in the same class.

On its debut seven years previously, Concorde's graceful lines excited admiration while its retractable drooping nose fascinated. Its only potential competitor, the Soviet Tu-144, had crashed very publicly at the Paris Air Show; it was known as 'Concordski' because it so obviously imitated the Concorde. Rumour had it that the Soviet designers had furtively got hold of the blueprints, but had misunderstood them.

America's hard-nosed regulators took their time before being satisfied about the noise and safety of Concorde; cynics said that they were pressed by the US aircraft manufacturers to block it, as they had no such plane on the stocks. High oil prices, among other factors, stunted the development of scheduled services but Concorde has been a boon for the busy, the rich and the famous crossing the Atlantic and has contributed significantly to the globalization of business. But how could it survive with fares 30 times the lowest in the market?

AND...

Political & general

Jan Death of Chou En-lai, Chinese premier.
Apr First democratic elections in Portugal for over 50 years; Mario Soares premier. James Callaghan replaces Harold Wilson as UK premier. Morocco and Mauritania annex phosphate-rich Spanish Sahara.
Jul Israeli commandos rescue 106 Jewish hostages hijacked to Entebbe.
Sep Death of Mao Tse-tung; enormous earthquake in Northern China with at least 500,000 killed.

Business & finance

Apr Genentech, biotechnology firm, established.
May Stephen Wozniak (aged 26) and Steven Jobs (21) start Apple Computer, pioneering personal computers.
Aug Mexico devalues peso, after 22 years linked to US dollar.
Sep Economic crisis in UK and Italy.
Dec 9.1% stake in Fiat acquired by Libyan Arab Foreign Bank for $415 million. Rupert Murdoch acquires *New York Post*.

'And if our decision is negative, do I have to return the model?'

'It's nice to see some *people still appreciate the value of a dollar.*'

'Call me a sentimental fool, but I still *worship the almighty dollar.*'

1977

THE ALMIGHTY DOLLAR

The quadrupling of oil prices stimulated inflation in the United States, much the world's largest consumer of energy. It also put a strain on the international value of the dollar, in which Americans had always had implicit faith. The newly rich oil producers tried taking other currencies for their oil, but the dollar was more convenient, because of its size and liquidity – just as long as they could get more dollars for each barrel of oil. By 1977 the dollar had fallen by a third compared to the Deutschemark and the yen over seven years.

The dollar held its own well against sterling; Britain's economic and financial crisis had recently forced it to ask the IMF for a massive $3.9 billion assistance package. It was by far the largest such appeal by an advanced nation and it came with humiliating conditions attached, though Italy was not far behind. Britain was being treated like a third world country; it was another nail in the coffin of Labour's reputation for economic management, for which it duly paid the electoral penalty.

But reduced dependence on imported energy would help both the dollar and sterling. The Trans-Alaska Pipeline had taken nearly ten years to build; it was the largest ever privately financed project and, in June, began deliveries of oil to continental United States from North America's largest oil field at Prudhoe Bay, Alaska. A quarter of a century later, it was supplying 17% of the nation's oil needs. In Britain, too, the discovery and production of oil in the North Sea promised better times to come.

AND...

Political & general

Jan Jimmy Carter President of USA.
Jun Blackout in New York emphasizes seriousness of energy crisis. First general election in Spain for over 40 years; Adolfo Suarez premier.
Jul 'Gang of Four' (including widow of Mao Tse-tung) disgraced in China; Deng Xiaoping resumes leadership role and plans reforms. Mohammed Zia Ul Haq deposes Pakistan Premier Zulfikar Ali Bhutto and imposes military rule.
Nov President Sadat of Egypt visits Israel on peace mission.

Business & finance

Apr Fraudulent losses of SF1.5 billion at Credit Suisse.
Jun Environmental controversy fails to prevent Trans-Alaska Pipeline from delivering oil to the rest of USA.
Sep Laker Airways launches cut-price transatlantic service 'Skytrain'.
Dec Germany and Japan attempt to ward off hot money, as their currencies rise against the US dollar.

'That's an excellent suggestion, Miss Triggs.
Perhaps one of the men here would like to make it.'

1978

THE GLASS CEILING

Despite the 1948 Universal Declaration of Human Rights, women continued to face discrimination. A few women reached the pinnacle of politics, usually owing their success to widowhood or daughterhood, such as Sirimavo Bandaranaike, Indira Gandhi or Argentina's Isabelita Perón, who not only took on her deceased husband's job, but also the aura of his previous wife, the charismatic Evita, darling of the masses.

In business there was still a 'glass ceiling' to thwart advancement for women; progress there was, but it was slow. In 1978 Midland Bank appointed Dame Rosemary Murray, a former vice chancellor of Cambridge University, to its board; it was the first UK clearing bank to take such a step. By then, many leading companies could boast of having at least one woman director. Often, however, this had the air of tokenism and many unreformed men were not prepared to take seriously a woman's contribution.

In the same year, Washington saw 100,000 marchers demanding an Equal Rights Amendment, 55 years after it first came up in Congress. Not much had changed since Simone de Beauvoir's comment about industry and politics in *The Second Sex* a generation previously: 'It is a world that still belongs to men.' Margaret Thatcher was soon to take centre stage, but she thought it more significant to be the first science graduate than the first woman to be prime minister of Britain.

AND...

Political & general

May Italian Premier, Aldo Moro, found killed after kidnapping by 'Red Brigade' terrorists.

Sep Camp David agreement set up by President Carter, between Israel and Egypt; 'framework for peace' in the Middle East. Election of Polish Pope, John Paul II, after deaths of Paul VI and John Paul I; promise of change in East Europe, especially Poland.

Sep Widespread demonstrations against the Shah in Iran, leading to oil prices being doubled by end of 1980 (second 'oil shock').

Dec USA and China resume diplomatic relations after interval of 30 years.

Business & finance

Apr Volkswagen's US plant begins producing Rabbit and becomes first foreign company to make small fuel-efficient cars; Japanese soon follow.

Jul Credit Suisse First Boston (CSFB), successor to investment bank Credit Suisse White Weld, set up.

Oct Kohlberg, Kravis & Roberts startles Wall Street with $380 million leveraged buy-out of Houdaille Industries – largest 'taking private' transaction to date.

Nov DM3 billion and SF2 billion 'Carter' bonds strengthen US dollar.

'Do you think the directors ever pretend to be us?'

'His last wish was that he shouldn't contribute
to the growing fuel shortage.'

'… and there will be a massive commitment of funds
to make petrol out of peanuts.'

1979

PETROL FROM PEANUTS

Instability in the Middle East triggered the second 'oil shock'. In January 1979, after widespread demonstrations, the Shah and his family fled Iran and the Ayatollah Khomeini returned from his exile in Paris to set up an Islamic Republic. There was a surge of popular hostility against America, the 'Great Satan', which was blamed for the corruption, brutality and irreligion of the Shah's regime – 52 US hostages were captured by the mob and incarcerated in Tehran for 444 days. It was a horrendous dilemma for the clever and idealistic President Carter, for which his previous experience as a peanut farmer and regional politician had not prepared him. Then came the Soviet invasion of Afghanistan. War between Iraq and Iran soon followed and the Cold War was back, despite those recent Helsinki Accords.

After some recovery after the first 'oil shock', recession and inflation again stalked the globe. Energy costs rose steeply, oil going from $14 to $35 a barrel. But OPEC was in disarray and the rest of the world was better prepared; prices were to fall back sharply a few years later. President Carter promoted the production of petrol from new sources, such as coal, shale or alcohol, and encouraged domestic oil exploration; he wanted to reduce dependence on the Middle East, where he had made heroic efforts to broker a peace between Israel and Egypt.

AND...

Political & general

Mar Three Mile Island nuclear power plant accident.

May After strikes, inflation and failed public services ('the winter of discontent'), Margaret Thatcher becomes first woman UK premier.

Jul Saddam Hussein becomes president of Iraq; initiates bloody purge of leading officials.

Aug Earl Mountbatten assassinated in Ireland by IRA.

Oct USA hands over canal to Panama. Ugandan despot Idi Amin deposed.

Nov After hostage seizure, USA freezes Iranian assets.

Dec Soviet invasion of Afghanistan.

Business & finance

Citibank and others develop interest rate swaps in London.

Mar European Monetary System and Exchange Rate Mechanism formally introduced, without UK participation; hopes of a 'zone of monetary stability'.

Jun Sony Walkman launched (over 200 million sold in next 20 years).

Aug Paul Volcker Chairman of the Federal Reserve Board; moves to curb inflation (13.3%) and protect dollar. New monetary policy hits markets badly ('Saturday Night Massacre') and spurs the growth of derivatives.

Oct End of UK foreign exchange controls helps City of London as global financial centre.

'Weight for weight, Louie, we'll still stick to narcotics.'

1980

A BARBAROUS RELIC

'You shall not press down upon the brow of labor this crown of thorns, you shall not crucify mankind upon a cross of gold' – William Jennings Bryan's passionate hostility to gold did not help him achieve the US presidency in 1896. Later, Keynes called it a 'barbarous relic', but gold remained a very popular medium for investment or decoration; it was also a pillar of the international monetary system and, for much of the 19th and early 20th centuries, most self-respecting currencies had to be on the Gold Standard.

After President Nixon uncoupled it from the US dollar, gold rose in value, though erratically. It was much in demand in unstable times, such as January 1980, as the Soviet Union was embarking on its doomed Afghan adventure; the gold price went from $475 an ounce to $850 and back to $481 in the space of a few weeks. These were heady figures compared to just $35 of ten years previously, but they were unsustainable and gold has rarely traded above $400 since. There was no rational way of forecasting its price, it yielded no income and it was costly to hold – it was certainly not an investment for widows and orphans, let alone mobsters.

AND...

Political & general

Mar Robert Mugabe president of Zimbabwe, formerly Southern Rhodesia.
Apr Failed attempt to rescue US hostages in Tehran.
May Death of President Tito of Yugoslavia; fears that the country would disintegrate, but it held together for 10 years. Referendum fails to support Quebec's secession from Canada.
Jul Moscow Olympics boycotted by 60 nations in protest at Soviet invasion of Afghanistan.
Aug Shipyard strike in Gdansk leads to liberalization in Poland; free trade unions permitted with the right to strike.
Sep Following border dispute, Iraq invades Iran; loss of OPEC cohesion and disruption of supplies.

Business & finance

Japan becomes world's largest car producer (7 million, compared to 20,000 in 1955).
Jan Federal loan guarantees save Chrysler, third largest US car-maker, from collapse.
Mar Depository Institutions Deregulation & Monetary Control Act makes level playing field for US banks. Failed attempt by Hunt brothers to corner silver.
Jun Midland Bank of UK announces plan to buy control of Crocker Bank, California; the ensuing problems led to Midland's loss of independence. Cable News Network (CNN) launched by Ted Turner.
Dec US prime rate reaches a high of 21.5%.

'When you say you have a terminal malfunction, Jackson, I trust you are speaking of yourself and not that five thousand pounds' worth of new hardware in your office.'

'Well, here we are with our personal computer, ready for any twists and
turns the conversation may take.'

'The world moves so fast nowadays.
It used to take years and years to become a confirmed horse's ass.'

1981

YOU CAN'T TEACH AN OLD MOUSE NEW CLICKS

The US Census Bureau acquired its first computer in 1951; it weighed 18 tons. Today, thanks to the silicon chip, you can carry the entire contents of your public library in the palm of your hand. The energy crisis encouraged cost savings devices at work, such as word processors, small computers and pocket calculators. In August 1981, the computer giant IBM belatedly spotted the trend and launched its own personal computer, giving it the acronym 'PC'; a tiny company called Microsoft provided its operating system.

Twenty years later, there were a billion computers around the world; many of them were 'IBM-compatible' personal computers, using Microsoft's system. They enabled instant communication between people everywhere, exemplifying Marshall McLuhan's description of the world as a 'global village'. They permitted access to the world's knowledge through the internet and opened up fabulous trading possibilities. Microsoft prospered hugely from this form of globalization; its market value became twice that of IBM and its founder, Bill Gates, the richest man in the world.

Poor IBM began to look like a corporate old fogey, too slow to save itself from the death of a thousand cuts, administered by a monstrous regiment of nerds and geeks. But, when all seemed lost, along came Lou Gerstner to rescue it in one of the most remarkable corporate recoveries ever, summed up in the title of his book, *Who Says Elephants Can't Dance?*

AND...

Political & general

Jan Ronald Reagan President of USA. Iran releases US hostages and recovers its frozen assets.
Feb Failed coup d'état attempt in Spain.
Mar Attempted assassination of Reagan.
May François Mitterrand President of France. Attempted assassination of Pope John Paul II.
Jun Israel destroys nuclear plant in Iraq.
Jul Marriage of Prince Charles and Lady Diana Spencer.
Sep First TGV train (Paris to Lyon).
Oct President Sadat of Egypt assassinated; succeeded by Hosni Mubarak.
Dec Martial law in Poland; Lech Walesa, union leader, arrested with supporters.

Business & finance

Global recession and energy efficiency reduces oil demand; price falls put pressure on heavily borrowed oil producers, like Mexico, who are also hit by highest ever US dollar interest rates.
Feb Rupert Murdoch buys *The Times* of London.
May Saudi Arabia lends SDR 8 billion to IMF, to enhance access to IMF funds for countries in payments difficulties.
Sep Poland's debt rescheduled; first indications of forthcoming international debt crisis.

'Good news. The Times *has upgraded us from*
a "junta" to a "military government".'

1982

OUR SON OF A BITCH DITCHED

Two centuries ago, Dr Johnson poured scorn on the Falkland Islands '...which not even the southern savages have dignified with habitation', but there was now a small, intensely patriotic British community. In April 1982, when Britain's attentions were elsewhere, Argentina seized the islands. President Leopoldo Galtieri thought it 'absolutely improbable' that Britain would respond with force, but he hadn't allowed for Margaret Thatcher's resolve; after the failure of diplomacy and the freezing of Argentina's assets, *La Tacher* sent a task force to recover the colony. It was her finest hour and she went on to win an election, while the junta crumbled in Buenos Aires.

Unable to service its $40 billion external debt, Argentina had shot itself in the foot; its troubles proved contagious and, by year's end, a general Latin American debt crisis was in full swing. But Argentinians could take some comfort in their defeat, because Raul Alfonsin was soon elected president democratically, though the economic performance remained miles below the potential of such a well-endowed country.

The Thatcher/Reagan era saw the spread of economic liberalism across South America; soon, almost all the dictators were gone. The 'son of a bitch', so beloved of the CIA in its struggle with communism, could now be ditched; the wretched Galtieri, despite President Reagan's recent description of him as a 'magnificent general', was thrown to the wolves and soon sent to jail. Sadly, the end of the dictators was not matched by an end to corruption.

AND...

Political & general

Jan Break-up of AT&T agreed with US government, after lawsuits on competition grounds.
Feb Nationalization of leading banks and other companies in France.
Jun Israeli invasion of Lebanon; PLO expelled from Beirut.
Aug King Fahad succeeds to Saudi throne.
Oct Helmut Kohl German Chancellor.
Felipe González socialist premier of Spain.
Nov Brezhnev dies; his successor, Yuri Andropov, passes functions to youngest Politburo member, Mikhail Gorbachev.

Business & finance

Jan First Japanese Eurobond with warrants; $130 billion such issues over 8 years.
Feb Mexico devalues, after capital flight.
Jun Security Pacific Bank buys 29.9% of Hoare Govett, London brokers; first of many such deals. Collapse of Banco Ambrosiano (fraud) and *July* of Penn Square Bank (energy loans).
Aug Mexico unable to meet its commitments.
Sep London International Financial Futures Exchange opens.
Dec IMF agrees rescue package for Mexico. Vodafone obtains first UK mobile phone licence.

'We could hold up the bank and take the money –
then the IMF will have to send more money,
so we hold up the bank and take the money ...'

*'But I bet if I were a Third World country
I'd never get a letter like this about my overdraft.'*

1983

COUNTRIES DON'T GO BANKRUPT

When the oil producers became really rich, they left much of their money on deposit with banks; the banks lent it on to countries that had to pay much more for their oil. But when Paul Volcker became Chairman of the Federal Reserve, his attempts to curb inflation resulted in sky-high interest rates in USA – the prime rate, having been around 6% to 8% in the three years before his appointment, spent the next six years in the 12% to 20% range, with a corresponding impact on international rates. This was tough on America, but a disaster for the rest of the globe; when America catches a cold, it's pneumonia for everyone else. So it was no wonder that one country after another could not make ends meet. First it was Poland, then Mexico, but Argentina's failed Falklands adventure made a general crisis unavoidable in Latin America and elsewhere.

The International Monetary Fund rode to the rescue and, by the end of 1983, had rescheduled the debts of 24 countries. 'Rescheduling' means lending a bit more for a bit longer and being kind-hearted about interest payments; it was a handy, if cynical, device to avoid the need for default, which confirmed the remark of Citibank's Walter Wriston that 'countries don't go bankrupt' – to which one wag responded, 'but the banks that lend to them do'. Heavy loan losses did indeed damage many banks, some fatally.

AND...

Political & general

Mar President Reagan proposes Strategic Defense Initiative ('Star Wars'). Emergence of Green Party as a significant force in Germany.
Jun The Pope visits his homeland, Poland; *Jul* martial law lifted there.
Aug Bettino Craxi first socialist premier of Italy.
Sep South Korean airliner, erroneously thought to be spying, shot down over Soviet Union; all aboard killed.
Nov After sale of US armaments, Donald Rumsfeld sent as presidential emissary to forge better relations with Iraq. Rauf Denktash declares independent state in Northern Cyprus.
Dec Raul Alfonsin elected president of Argentina.

Business & finance

Jan Robin Leigh-Pemberton succeeds Gordon Richardson as Governor of Bank of England.
Jul Deregulation of London Stock Exchange agreed with UK government.
Nov Michael Milken (of Drexel Burnham Lambert) proposes 'junk bonds' for takeover deals; Mesa Petroleum uses them to bid for Gulf Oil Corporation, 30 times its size.

'Then, of course, there'll be the usual search fee.'

1984

LEGAL EAGLES

The medieval scrivener charged by the word, while the traditional family lawyer charged by the hour or according to a tariff – methods which tended to increase the level of fees, with no incentive for efficiency. But their fees are nothing compared to the earnings of entrepreneurial lawyers in class actions, personal injury or bankruptcy cases. When Texaco disrupted Pennzoil's acquisition of Getty Oil in 1984, the ensuing case landed Texaco temporarily in the bankruptcy courts, from which it emerged $3 billion worse off, while $400 million was said to have gone to the lawyers.

Litigiousness is part of the American way of life, but lawyers in London were also prospering hugely from the cross-border business that was inherent in the process of globalization. When a German bank arranged a loan to China, or a Japanese bank managed a bond issue for an Italian company, it was likely to be arranged in London, in the English language and under English law. When the international debt crisis shook the world in the eighties, lawyers were ever present in the rescheduling process; but their own fees were usually paid, promptly and unrescheduled.

AND...

Political & general

Jan AT&T divests itself of 22 'Baby Bells'; increased competition in the US telecom sector.

Feb Death of Soviet leader Yuri Andropov, succeeded by Konstantin Chernenko, with Mikhail Gorbachev effectively his deputy.

Mar Start of 12-month coal miners' strike in UK.

Jun Pierre Trudeau resigns after 16 years (with one brief interruption) as Canadian premier.

Sep UK agrees to return Hong Kong to China in 1997.

Oct Indian Premier Indira Gandhi assassinated; succeeded by her son Rajiv. Bomb attack by IRA on Mrs Thatcher and other UK politicians in Brighton.

Business & finance

May Continental Illinois, eighth largest US bank, rescued by US government, after real estate, energy and third world loan losses; deposit gathering had been impeded by state branching restrictions.

Oct Johnson Matthey Bankers rescued by Bank of England.

Nov £3.9 billion privatization of British Telecom in UK, managed by Kleinwort Benson; 12 other major privatizations follow in UK, which provides advisory services on privatization to many other countries.

Dec Worst-ever industrial accident at Union Carbide pesticide plant in Bhopal, India; 2,000 killed.

'It was 1961. Boom times, stability, easy credit ... and, of course, none of the other entering classmen at law school thought of specializing in insolvency cases.'

'I say buy up Sony and Honda, and so forth. I mean, tit for tat.'

'I just hope I can make it big before all the van Goghs are gone.'

1985

JAPAN'S GLOBAL SHOPPING SPREE

Japan was better than most in adjusting to the energy crisis. In 1985, its huge trade surplus pushed the yen 20% up against the dollar; its investment banks grabbed 40% of the international bond market and its commercial banks became the world's biggest. Japanese investors combed the world for glamorous assets. One van Gogh painting went to Japan for $40 million, another for twice that – prices not seen before or since. American crown jewels, such as Columbia Pictures and the Rockefeller Center, fell to Japanese purchasers.

But it was one-way business. An American entrepreneur, Boone Pickens, bought 26% of car parts maker Koito. Although the largest shareholder, Pickens was denied a seat on the board – why should a foreigner poke his nose into Koito's delicate ownership and trading ties with the likes of Toyota? Selling was equally difficult and Japan was recalcitrant in allowing fair access to its home markets.

Tokyo stocks quadrupled over five years, but the bubble burst on the last day of the eighties. The market fell 75% over 12 years and the economy seemed to go into irreversibly stagnant mode – an astonishing outcome after four decades of stellar progress. But Japan had re-invented itself after the Meiji Restoration in 1868 and after its defeat in World War II. Doubtless it would do so again. There were promising signs – Japan became the biggest foreign investor and aid donor, had the highest savings rate and balance of payments surplus and was dominant in several high-tech industries. Perhaps Japan could afford to look beyond the doldrums of the stock market and the parlous state of its banks.

AND...

Political & general

Jan Jacques Delors president of the European Commission. Tancredo Nieves first civilian president in Brazil since 1964.
Mar Gorbachev becomes Soviet leader, launches *perestroika* (change and development) and *glasnost* (openness).
May Nature magazine describes large ozone layer hole.
Nov Cordial first Gorbachev–Reagan summit in Geneva. Anglo-Irish Agreement on the future of Northern Ireland. Abu Nidal terrorist attacks at Rome and Vienna airports.

Business & finance

Apr New formula for Coke outrages customers; old formula soon reintroduced.
May Rupert Murdoch acquires Twentieth Century Fox and becomes US citizen.
Sep Plaza Accord to depress strong US dollar.
Oct US Treasury Secretary Baker proposes to help indebted third world countries through market techniques.
Nov Microsoft launches Windows operating system.

'I'm sending the wife and family to the country for the Big Bang.'

1986

THE END OF A CLUB

The London Stock Exchange was like a gentleman's club, with the odd female member. New York had been deregulated a decade earlier, while Tokyo was making heady progress – London had cold-shouldered the Eurobond market and risked being left behind in the global securities business. Under government pressure, it abandoned its cosy system of fixed commissions. Soon brokers, jobbers and merchant banks were thrown together and acquired by multinational banks. The day of impact, in October 1986, was 'Big Bang'. A new regulatory structure was created, mainly to protect the small investor and ensure fair dealing. Big Bang made many members millionaires and confirmed London as a major financial centre; it also signalled a big transfer abroad of the City's ownership.

At first there were too many players. Where there had been two large and six small UK government bond dealers there were now 27; £100 million of private capital was replaced by £700 million of institutional capital. Yet the size of the canvas was unchanged, about £165 billion, and there was no increase in the number of experienced dealers (some of the best ones departed the scene to enjoy their sudden wealth). It was the same for equities, although Britain's privatization policy and the rise of global equities yielded bigger opportunities. Inevitably, some banks lost all that they had invested in London's securities business. For them, 'Big Bang' blew a big hole in their finances.

AND...

Political & general

Jan Spain and Portugal join the EEC. UK and France agree to build tunnel under the Channel.

Feb Under popular pressure, Marcos gives way to Corazon Aquino as Philippine president. Single European Act to remove trade barriers in Europe.

Apr Chernobyl reactor explodes. US air strike on Libya.

Oct Second Reagan–Gorbachev summit at Reykjavik; disagreement on Star Wars.

Nov Iran-Contra affair comes to light in USA; illegal arms deals with Iran and Nicaragua involving senior US officials.

Business & finance

Jan Rupert Murdoch introduces new computerized printing machinery at Wapping.

Feb Midland Bank sells interest in Crocker Bank, California; estimated loss £1 billion.

Apr Illegal share support deals help Distillers buy Guinness; four were later jailed for role in scandal.

Jul Oil $7.20 a barrel.

Oct Yamani replaced as Saudi Oil Minister, after 24 years.

Aug Sumitomo Bank 12.5% stake in Goldman Sachs.

Nov Liquidity crisis in the Floating Rate Note market; huge Eurobond losses.

'I won't be able to handle your account any more,
as it suddenly appears that you're a small investor.'

ANIMAL SPIRITS RAMPANT, 1987–2002

What Keynes called the 'animal spirits' of capitalism were back with a vengeance in the era of Margaret Thatcher and Ronald Reagan. Trade, investment and speculation surged around the world, with much help from the new technology – computer prices were falling 12% per annum. Business was fashionable again and successful entrepreneurs and financiers, so often pariahs in the past, were lionized. Globalization seemed to be sweeping everything before it.

The most durable obstacle had been the Iron Curtain, but its visible symbol, the Berlin Wall, was quickly knocked over by the German people, yearning for reunification. In the twinkling of an eye, the mighty Soviet empire was gone and more than a dozen new countries had arisen from the ashes. Since their own economic philosophy had utterly failed, these new countries seized on the Anglo-Saxon model as the only available alternative. The City of London taught them how to privatize their state industries, while the titans of American finance and academia rushed around the globe to build new economies from scratch.

But it came at a high price. Since the new systems had to be built overnight to prevent economic collapse, corners were cut. Poor Mother Russia was raped to within an inch of her life, while the new elite vastly enriched itself. Hot money, a key component of the Anglo-Saxon model, did serious damage to South East Asian and other countries.

Matching the spread of globalization was the spread of protest. Often organized on a global basis, and aided by modern technology, protest came in all shapes and sizes. At one end of the spectrum were the fanatics who carried out the 9/11 outrages; at the other end, Ralph Nader, now almost part of the establishment, was able to have a shot at the US presidency. The new century opened with a crisis of capitalism as equity markets fell for three years in a row and the good name of business was besmirched by lurid scandals.

'I'm perfectly willing to suffer the slings and arrows
as long as I can keep the outrageous fortune.'

'Miss Smith, buy up the rights to the Bible and get that part changed about the rich man and the eye of the needle.'

1987

LUNCH IS FOR WIMPS

A career in finance or business was now quite respectable. A hundred graduates applied for every City vacancy and young doctors and dentists abandoned their professions for stockbroking, as London's All Share Index tripled, helped by the euphoria of deregulation. The Dow Jones doubled in the mid-eighties and the Tokyo market was rampant, until the crash of October 1987 ended the fun – for a while.

It was again fashionable to acquire and flaunt riches. Morality might have to go by the board once in a while; when arbitrageur Ivan Boesky told Berkeley students that 'greed is healthy', he was lustily applauded. Gordon Gekko, hero of the 1987 film *Wall Street*, epitomized the new entrepreneur who profits from insider dealing but has no use for old world courtesies like a friendly chat over a good lunch.

But greed can slither into crime and the gloss rather went off Boesky's philosophy when he was sent to jail for an insider dealing scandal, in which some leading Wall Street figures were implicated. It also provided an example of the globalization of insider dealing, since he fingered some financiers in London who had illegally manipulated the shares of Guinness during its acquisition of Distillers. Four of them went to jail, though others evaded detection by concealing their deals through the ever-friendly Swiss banking system.

AND...

Political & general

Feb Bettino Craxi, longest serving (3½ years) Italian premier, resigns.
Apr Quebec recognized as a 'distinct society' by provincial premiers in Canada. Portugal agrees handover of Macao to China in 1999.
Nov Moscow's communist party chief Boris Yeltsin sacked.
Dec Reagan–Gorbachev agreement in Washington on large-scale US and Soviet destruction of missiles. Intifada; uprising of Palestinians in West Bank and Gaza. 338 convicted at mafia trial in Palermo.

Business & finance

Feb Louvre Accord; G-7 finance ministers agree to stabilize currencies.
Mar Chrysler buys American Motors, leaving 3 major US motor manufacturers.
May Citibank's $3 billion reserve against third world debt portfolio causes other banks to follow suit.
Jun Alan Greenspan succeeds Paul Volcker as Federal Reserve Chairman.
Oct Stock market crash in the midst of equity offer of £7.3 billion of BP shares for UK government; Kuwait snaps up 21.7% stake, but forced to reduce it to 10%. Nomura of Japan ranked top Eurobond manager.

'My father told me, "neither a borrower nor a lender be", and I have always followed that advice. That's probably been my trouble.'

1988

CONSUMER CONFIDENCE

'Neither a borrower nor a lender be' was the advice that Polonius gave to his son Laertes. It was doubtless appropriate in the mythical Denmark of Shakespeare's *Hamlet*, but it would bring today's open economies grinding to a halt. His maxim that 'borrowing dulls the edge of husbandry' is still all too true, but was far from the minds of British house buyers as they chased house prices to giddy heights in 1988, just as it was an alien concept to credit card junkies all over the world.

Good husbandry was also forgotten by American savings and loan associations, costing them their right to be known as 'thrifts'. When President Carter brought in the Depository Institutions Deregulation and Monetary Control Act, eight years previously, it was supposed to create a level playing field for banks and thrifts; but for some thrifts it was altogether too level and there was nothing to stop their dash for the exotic corners of the field – why stick with lending on bricks and mortar? Why not feast at the global banquet and play the oil market? Eventually Uncle Sam had to pick up the tab; the cost of rescuing the thrifts was estimated at over $315 billion.

Yet borrowing is a great creator of a nation's wealth today, as long as there is confidence in its economy, its currency and its financial institutions.

AND...

Political & general

Feb Dispute between Azeris and Armenians in Soviet Union over Nagorno Karabakh.
Mar Ceausescu plans destruction of 8,000 Romanian villages and relocation of inhabitants to towns. Saddam Hussein drops chemicals on Halabja, Kurdish village; 5,000 killed.
Jul Ayatollah Khomeini accepts end of Iran–Iraq war (he calls it 'worse than taking poison'); huge human and economic losses, with no gain for either side.
Aug President Zia Ul Haq of Pakistan killed in air crash; *Nov* Benazir Bhutto premier.
Oct Baltic republics try to secede from Soviet Union.
Dec Armenian earthquake; 50,000 killed. 270 killed by terrorists in Lockerbie air crash.

Business & finance

Mar UK personal tax cuts fuels housing boom and consumer spending.
Jul Basel Capital Accord sets 8% capital adequacy ratio for banks.
Oct BCCI and ten employees indicted in Florida for money laundering.
Dec $25 billion acquisition of RJR Nabisco, using junk bonds, with help of Drexel Burnham Lambert, which is fined $650 million for its securities activities and goes into bankruptcy 14 months later.

'… and please hurry. My credit card expires at midnight.'

'My country doesn't understand me.'

1989

A NASTY LITTLE MEETING

Britain continued to have an uneasy relationship with its European neigh-bours, at both personal and political levels. At first, Britain did not join the Exchange Rate Mechanism (ERM), whose common currency was the Euro-pean Currency Unit (ECU), forerunner of the euro. But, in April 1989, Jacques Delors, president of the European Commission, unveiled his detailed plan to create economic and monetary union in Europe. Many in Britain distrusted this rush towards European union, preferring de Gaulle's conception of a *Europe des patries*, where each nation maintained its own distinct personality.

The British Prime Minister, Margaret Thatcher, was put under intense pressure to join the ERM by Chancellor of the Exchequer Nigel Lawson and Foreign Secretary Geoffrey Howe, both of whom threatened to resign if she didn't play ball; at a 'nasty little meeting' she reluctantly accepted the prin-ciple of joining, but at some future, unspecified date. In due course, both Lawson and Howe resigned, while Britain did indeed join the ERM. It was an unhappy end to power for an outstanding Prime Minister; like her friend, Mikhail Gorbachev, she was more appreciated abroad than at home.

AND...

Political & general

Jan George Bush President of USA.
Feb Last Soviet troops leave Afghanistan.
Jun Iranian leader, Khomeini, dies, succeeded by Rafsanjani. Demonstrations crushed in Tiananmen Square, Beijing.
Aug Ethnic unrest at the fringes of the Soviet Union. General breakdown of communist regimes in East Europe.
Sep Lebanese reconciliation agreed in Taif, Saudi Arabia.
Nov Berlin Wall torn down. John Williamson's 'Washington Consensus'; policy of introducing free markets globally.
Dec Chile and Brazil elect civilian presidents. USA ousts General Noriega, Panamanian leader, and brings him to USA for trial. Gorbachev and Bush signify end of Cold War at Malta summit (as had Brezhnev in 1973).

Business & finance

Feb London Borough of Hammersmith & Fulham dealt in £3.3 billion swaps, beyond legal powers; large losses for banks.
Mar Exxon Valdez pours 11 million gallons of oil into Alaskan waters. US Treasury Secretary Brady proposes IMF help for heavily indebted countries.
Apr Delors Report recommends approach to European Economic & Monetary Union.
Jul Leveraged buy-out attempt on BAT Industries.
Nov Major US acquisitions by Japan – Rockefeller Center and Columbia Pictures. Deutsche Bank buys Morgan Grenfell, damaged by Guinness scandal.
Dec Bank of Japan raises interest rates; 48% fall in stock market over next 9 months, from all-time high.

'That's where the Commies have the edge on us –
they don't have to worry about the Dow-Jones index.'

1990

WALL STREET COMES TO RED SQUARE

As Europe moved remorselessly towards economic and monetary union, the Soviet Union was unravelling. In June 1990 came the killer punch, when Boris Yeltsin declared independence for The Russian Federation. Other Soviet republics did likewise. Russians quickly threw away Karl Marx's *Das Kapital* and taught themselves all the tricks of global capitalism – and a few more besides. Under the influence of the IMF and Anglo-American high finance, a 'shock therapy' of privatization and deregulation was ruthlessly applied to the creaking economy. Huge fortunes were made as state companies were sold for a song to favoured oligarchs, in return for loans to shore up the government; apparatchiks became owners of the factories that they managed; ordinary Russians could go into business without fear of being branded as wreckers and shipped off to the gulag.

Emulating the Arabs of the seventies and the Japanese of the eighties, Russians took centre stage as global exporters of capital, pumping $300 billion into Western property, banking, stock and art markets – much of it virtually stolen from the state. Stock exchanges sprang up from St Petersburg to Vladivostok, but the economy collapsed by 50% in the 1990s and many looked back nostalgically to the communist era; Russians were now much poorer and less secure, but at least they had a measure of freedom and democracy. It was galling for them to peer at their great rival beyond the Pamirs and the Gobi; instead of tearing down the rotten Marxist edifice, China injected it with capitalist yeast and, after ten years, had lifted its GDP from 40% below Russia's to 60% above it.

AND...

Political & general

Feb Nelson Mandela released from jail.
May Burmese election result annulled by military regime.
Aug Kuwait invaded by Iraq; leads to Gulf War.
Oct German re-unification. In Rome, EEC pressure for closer union dismissed by UK Premier Margaret Thatcher as 'cloud cuckoo land'.
Nov Thatcher is deposed, declaring 'it's a funny old world', and is replaced by John Major.
Dec Lech Walesa president of Poland and Slobodan Milosevic president of Serbia.

Business & finance

Jun Treuhandanstalt set up to conduct privatization of former East German companies; Russia and former Soviet satellites initiate privatization policies.
Oct UK joins the Exchange Rate Mechanism. Gulf War triggers oil price rise, but fears of a third 'oil shock' not realized.

'We've a problem with this aid cheque. Who do we make it payable to –
USSR, Soviet Union, Commonwealth of Russian ...?'

'Well, it all depends. Where are these huddled masses coming from?'

1991

QUIETER RESTAURANTS

The whole world loves its mobile phone. Rich countries enjoy lots of new services and appreciate ending the old state telephone monopoly while poor countries can quickly establish a phone network without lots of wires, posts and cables. The mobile phone is indeed a wonderful fruit from the garden of globalization.

Norman Lamont, British Chancellor of the Exchequer, disagreed. He judged the mobile phone 'one of the greatest scourges of modern life' and taxed it in his 1991 budget, in the vain hope that 'restaurants will be quieter and the roads will be safer'. But, like the ancient English king, Canute, he could not stop the tide and the number of mobile phone subscribers around the world rose from 20 million to a billion in 10 years. Weeks after Lamont's budget, Vodafone was spun off from Racal and soon became the largest company in Europe, with over 100 million customers.

Nine years later, another Chancellor, Gordon Brown, sold new UK phone licences to five telecom companies for £22 billion. His timing was brilliant, with the NASDAQ Composite Index, laden with telecom stocks, near its peak, but it turned out to be a huge burden on the companies; their shares came tumbling down as they tried to reduce debts built up during the scramble for global dominance. It would indeed be a pyrrhic victory should any of the companies have to give up the licences so expensively won, with the subsequent reduction in competition.

AND...

Political & general

Jan 'Desert Storm' to free Kuwait.

Mar Warsaw Pact dissolved.

May Rajiv Gandhi, Indian premier, assassinated.

Jun Yugoslavia fragments; Croatia and Serbia go to war. Boris Yeltsin elected president of Russia in free election.

Aug Hardliner coup in Moscow, from alarm at Gorbachev's policies, suppressed with Yeltsin's help.

Dec Maastricht Treaty, towards a more unified Europe. End of Soviet Union; Gorbachev resigns. Yeltsin appoints Deputy Premier Yegor Gaidar to launch market reforms in Russia.

Business & finance

Apr European Bank for Reconstruction and Development set up; much criticized for its extravagant management. UK council tax replaces community charge ('poll tax'), a controversial tax, introduced by Margaret Thatcher.

Jul Fraudulent bank, BCCI, closed down.

Nov Robert Maxwell's apparent suicide; huge fraud uncovered in his media business and pension funds. Wal-Mart begins overseas expansion in Mexico.

Dec PAN AM airline, founded in 1927, closes down.

'I'm looking for a hedge against my hedge funds.'

1992

THE MAN WHO BROKE THE BANK OF ENGLAND

A 'hedge' suggests insurance against loss, but to most hedge fund managers this objective is much too boring. Instead, they have become freewheeling adventurers of markets in every corner of the globe. No activity was out of bounds, as shown by George Soros – 'the man who broke the Bank of England' – when he helped drive sterling out of the Exchange Rate Mechanism in September 1992; his task was made much easier by hints from Germany's central bank, the Bundesbank ('the gang leaders of Europe', as they liked to call themselves), that sterling was overvalued.

In fact, Britain's humiliating exit from the ERM was a blessing in disguise and its economy prospered as never before. Brits could be forgiven for feeling a certain *schadenfreude* as the mighty Bundesbank became an outhouse of the new European Central Bank and Germany inherited the 'sick man of Europe' title so often slung at Britain in the past. Margaret Thatcher's outspoken hostility to European federalism and all its works had led to her fall from power but her doubts about British membership of the ERM were well founded; how could it be right for sterling, erstwhile proud currency of the world, to be shackled to such a rickety structure?

AND...

Political & general

Mar Violent clashes in Sarajevo as Bosnia is sucked into Yugoslav civil war.
Apr Contrary to expectations, UK Premier John Major leads Conservatives to fourth successive election victory. Manuel Noriega, former Panamanian president, is convicted in a US court and jailed for money laundering and drug smuggling.
Jun Earth Summit in Brazil to discuss condition of the globe; limited progress made. The Danish people reject Maastricht Treaty in a referendum while the French people narrowly accept it.
Dec US troops sent to Somalia on humanitarian mission, after civil war, in which 300,000 perished.

Business & finance

Lloyd's of London has its largest one year loss of £2 billion; many members suffer intensely, because of their unlimited liability.
Jul HSBC acquires balance of shares in Midland Bank not already owned by it. Russia suffers from hyper-inflation, joins the IMF.
Sep Britain's withdrawal from the Exchange Rate Mechanism; sterling falls and floats, improving Britain's prospects while at the same time the Italian lira also leaves ERM. Extreme divergence of interest rates pushes US dollar to all-time low against Deutschemark.

139

'And this is the space for Mrs Thatcher's dead body.'

'My father wanted me to go into his insurance business and I wanted to go into the theatre, so we compromised.'

'Don't even bother reading the fine print.
We've included it merely for the sake of tradition.'

1993

LIME STREET BLUES

Most insurance companies pursued a pretty uneventful course – apart from Lloyd's of London. This unique institution did so well that it built a superb building in Lime Street and recruited many new underwriting members or 'Names'. Traditionally, members had been resident in Britain, but Lloyd's caught the global bug in a big way and trawled the world for new members. Most of these individuals did not work at Lloyd's but trustfully underwrote its risks, the size and nature of which were not usually explained to them, even in the fine print. With increased membership numbers came extra under-writing capacity and it was inevitable that there would be a higher degree of risk in the business; some underwriters were not above keeping the best for themselves and passing on the worst to their Names.

By 1993 Lloyd's had lost £8 billion over five years from reckless expan-sion, unprecedented disasters and huge asbestos judgements. Lloyd's sur-vived, but not before appalling losses had fallen on Names; many of them lost their homes and possessions by virtue of the unlimited liability carried by members of Lloyd's.

AND...

Political & general

Jan Bill Clinton president of the USA.
'Velvet divorce' as Czechoslovakia split into two nations.
Feb Terrorist attack on World Trade Center, New York; 6 killed and 1,000 injured.
Queen Elizabeth II of UK agrees to pay tax.
Bettino Craxi, former premier, in huge corruption scandal in Italy 'Tangentopoli' – goes into Tunisian exile.
May Danish referendum; narrow vote for Maastricht Treaty.
Jul UNO warns of threat of large migrations.
Sep Oslo Accords; hope of Palestinian-Israeli settlement.
Oct Violent clash between President Yeltsin and Russian parliament. Nobel Peace Prize for Nelson Mandela and FW de Klerk for dismantling apartheid.
Nov Maastricht Treaty in force; the EEC becomes the European Union.
Dec Downing Street Declaration lays out peace plan for Northern Ireland.

Business & finance

Jun Euro Disney opens, near Paris; initial results disappointing.
Jul Eddie George succeeds Robin Leigh-Pemberton as Governor of Bank of England.
Aug Speculative pressures cause suspension of European Rate Mechanism; currencies fluctuate within broad band of 15%.
Dec After 7 years, 'Uruguay Round' trade talks concluded, with revised GATT, to stimulate world trade; leads to formation of World Trade Organization (WTO).

*'I see it as a golden opportunity for you
to tighten your stranglehold on me.'*

1994

AN ENGLISHMAN'S HOME IS HIS CASTLE

In 1994 the British housing market was in the fourth year of a nasty depression, made all the more painful by the excesses of the late eighties boom years; nonetheless, the market had still almost doubled in ten years and would soon resume its rise. More than their European brethren, the British dreamed of owning their own homes. If you could get the right mortgage at the right time, you could be rich – provided you were able to service it. Money released from the housing market stimulated the economy, but distorted it and stoked inflation.

In London, prices were especially high, as people from all over the globe bought properties for rent, holidays or protection against bad times back home; for many, it was the first and only investment that they made outside their home country. A Londoner could trade his one-room flat in Chelsea for a castle in France, but what would happen to London if policemen, doctors, nurses or firemen could not afford to live there?

AND...

Political & general

Jan Huge earthquake in Los Angeles.
Mar US troops withdraw from Somalia, after local groups accept peace agreement.
Apr Genocidal massacres in Rwanda; 800,000 (mainly) Tutsis killed, over 3 million people displaced.
May Nelson Mandela president of South Africa, heading a multiracial government. Sudden death of John Smith, UK Labour leader; Tony Blair succeeds him.
Sep USA sends 20,000 troops to restore elected government in Haiti.
Dec Russia attacks breakaway republic of Chechnya.

Business & finance

Jan NAFTA trade agreement between Canada, USA and Mexico, where it is violently resisted as 'a death certificate for the indigenous peoples'.
Feb Higher US dollar interest rates hit global bond markets; big losses for investment banks after 1993's big profits.
Apr Heads of 7 companies deny tobacco's addictive nature in Washington; huge pressures to compensate victims.
May Channel Tunnel opened between UK and France.
Dec MERCOSUR South American trade agreement. Orange County loses $1.6 billion from derivatives; one of several organizations to suffer such losses. Mexico suffers massive capital flight; $51 billion rescue by IMF.

'You thought we would offer lower fares? How insensitive.'

'No offence meant, m'sieurs, but where you've designed your lovely kitchen area, we at Laker could squeeze in half-a-dozen extra seats.'

'And keep your eye on this little light at all times.
If it blinks out it means the airline has gone bankrupt.'

1995

NO FRILLS

Freddie Laker became a British folk hero for offering cheap transatlantic flights until the big boys put him out of business – but he was ahead of his time. South West Airlines became the fourth largest US airline with its no frills policies and sensitivity to customer wishes. Similar policies in Europe brought success to easyJet, founded in 1995, Ryanair and Go.

In 2001, Go, a British Airways subsidiary, was sold – it did 'not fit with our full service strategy'. But after the 9/11 terrorist attacks, it was the no frills boys that prospered; national carriers, such as Swissair and Sabena, collapsed, while US airlines had to plead for federal support. BA had some explaining to do when Go was sold on to easyJet for £374 million, over three times its recent sale price. With the no frills upstarts on one side and new airlines from younger nations – such as Emirates and Singapore – on the other side, the dear old national flag carriers were having a rough time.

It was a puzzling industry. Airlines were at the heart of globalization, yet how could they survive if they kept losing money? Warren Buffett, the legendary Omaha investor, remarked that 'despite putting in billions and billions and billions of dollars, the net return to owners from being in the entire airline industry, if you owned it all, and if you put up all this money, is less than zero'. Airline shares, like railroads, are usually in the dog-house, but new lambs always come forward for the slaughter. Perhaps the no frills formula would be a durable winner.

AND...

Political & general

Jan Sweden, Austria and Finland join European Union, Norway having declined. Kobe earthquake kills 6,000 people and destroys 100,000 houses.
Apr Terrorist attack in Oklahoma City kills 168.
May Jacques Chirac succeeds Mitterrand as French president.
Nov Yitzhak Rabin assassinated by young opponent of negotiations with the Palestinians. President Clinton visits Northern Ireland to help peace process.
Dec Dayton Accords aim to bring peace to Bosnia.

Business & finance

Jan Formal launch of World Trade Organization.
Feb Baring Brothers & Co bankrupted by fraudulent derivative losses.
May Swiss Banking Corp buys SG Warburg & Co, its strength and credibility much weakened.
Aug Flotation of Netscape, internet browser firm – huge following for this and similar stocks. Russian banks lend money to government, thereby getting shares in state enterprises on very advantageous terms.

'I think it's our duty to notify the feds, Kelly.'

1996

OFF TO THE LAUNDRY

No global business has grown like money laundering; greatly facilitated by technology and deregulation, it is estimated to amount to over $300 billion a year. It is how drug dealers, gangsters, terrorists, crooked politicians, embezzlers and undesirables of all sorts hide their ill-gotten gains and evade the tax man. One bank, BCCI, was built on the business, but went undetected for years; among its collaborators was Manuel Noriega, Panama's president, who was sent to a US jail for money laundering and drug smuggling.

Many perfectly respectable banks are unintentionally involved in money laundering, which is often hard to spot. One such bank was Bank of New York, which had been set up by one of America's founding fathers, Alexander Hamilton, back in 1784; he met his fate at the hands of Aaron Burr, a Chase Manhattan Bank founder, in a duel – bankers have always been very competitive! Bank of New York was a truly venerable institution, yet it was, from 1996 to 1999, unknowingly involved in laundering over $7 billion of Russian money – a tiny proportion of the funds that have poured out of Russia, to the great detriment of its economy and its people. Its experience highlighted the difficulties of keeping up with the launderers.

AND...

Political & general

Feb IRA bomb in Canary Wharf, London's new financial district; later, another in Manchester.

Mar Tension off Taiwan, as China tests missiles, provoking deployment of US aircraft carriers in the area.

May Benjamin Netanyahu premier of Israel; doubts about the peace process.

Jul Birth in Edinburgh of Dolly the sheep, first mammal to be cloned from an adult animal cell.

Aug Yeltsin re-elected president of Russia with big majority, thwarting communist resurgence. Prince Charles and Princess Diana divorce.

Oct Taleban regime in control of Kabul, Afghanistan.

Business & finance

Jan Conglomerates go out of fashion; UK/US group Hanson demerged into four separate focused companies and split of ITT, which had been built up through acquisitions in 1960s and 1970s. Merger forms Bank of Tokyo-Mitsubishi, largest bank in the world at the time.

Dec Fed Chairman Alan Greenspan warns against 'irrational exuberance' in equity markets. Boeing and McDonnell Douglas announce merger to create largest global aerospace company. Russia raises $1 billion through Eurobond; first such transaction since 1917.

'For Pete's sake, that's not what we meant by laundering drug money!'

'You're right! There are no women on the Joint Chiefs of Staff –
I can't believe I never noticed that!'

'They say that if she starts playing with her earrings you're dead.'

'First off, forget I'm a woman.'

1997

FORGET I'M A WOMAN

By the end of the century, a few women had reached the pinnacle of politics, business and the professions. None was more remarkable than Margaret Thatcher, the grocer's daughter from Grantham, who, as British Prime Minister, drove through liberal economic strategies in her own country and helped launch them around the world, with support from her kindred spirit in the White House, Ronald Reagan. The global spread of her economic policies helped bring down the dictatorships of right and left, thus adding to the welfare of humanity as a whole – so long as democracy could take root in alien territory.

In many businesses, women were successful, particularly in the new economy; they were more likely to get to the top in the media or travel than in a coal mine or iron foundry. Two thirds of boards in America and Britain had a female member, but few major companies had a woman in the chief executive's office, until Marjorie Scardino was appointed head of the British media group Pearson in 1997. Two years later, the US computer company, Hewlett-Packard, appointed Carly Fiorina as its chief executive officer. But they were the exceptions that proved the rule; the glass ceiling was still there to block promotion and equal pay was still not universal.

'Women hold up half the sky,' said Mao Tse-tung, but they certainly don't hold down half the top jobs.

AND...

Political & general

Mar Unrest in Albania; refugees flood into Italy. Widespread movements of people from East to West Europe.

May Labour wins UK election, with Tony Blair as premier. Mohammed Khatami elected president of Iran with 70% plurality but reforms made difficult by entrenched clerics holding many levers of power.

Jul Hong Kong formally handed over by UK to China.

Aug Princess Diana killed in car crash in Paris.

Dec Kyoto protocol on global warming; accepted by most nations except USA.

Business & finance

Merger activity among investment banks, as convergence between commercial and investment banks gathers pace.

Apr WTO negotiations to liberalize financial services.

May Gordon Brown, new Labour Chancellor of the Exchequer, changes Bank of England's role.

Aug Financial crisis engulfs East Asia; withdrawal of hot money an important factor. IMF provides $117 billion help. Arthur Andersen, largest auditing firm, plans demerger of its consultancy arm.

Dec US Department of Justice injunction on Microsoft on anti-trust considerations.

'Good grief! You're both alarmingly young for auditors. I trust you're acquainted with accepted corporate accounting principles.'

1998

THEN THERE WERE FIVE

First there were the 'Big Eight' accountancy firms, then the 'Big Six'; by 1998, they were almost the 'Big Four', but instead became the 'Big Five' when a merger was aborted. Accountants had always been seen as clever, unobtrusive and honest folk, crunching the numbers in a back room and dispensing sound advice. You'd be quite happy, though not necessarily thrilled, if your daughter wanted to marry one.

But globalization and competition had made the business much more exciting; clients expected 'creative accounting'. Vice President Cheney, in a previous incarnation as Halliburton Company boss, was quoted as complimenting the auditors for their work 'over and above the normal, by-the-books auditing arrangement'. Conflicts of interest abounded, particularly between the auditing and consultancy arms of accountancy firms. It was worrying that the audited accounts of several failed banks and companies gave no inkling of anything amiss. The biggest shock came four years later when a Houston court's guilty verdict forced one of the 'Big Five', Arthur Andersen, out of business because of its role in the Enron collapse.

AND...

Political & general

Mar Clashes between Serbs and Kosovo Liberation Army.

Apr Good Friday Agreement; renewed effort to bring peace to Northern Ireland.

May President Suharto deposed in Indonesia. Tension between India and Pakistan, as both nations announce nuclear bomb testing plans.

Aug Terrorist attacks on US embassies in Nairobi and Dar es Salaam.

Sep Gerhard Schröder succeeds Helmut Kohl as German Chancellor.

Oct General Pinochet arrested in London, at request of Spanish court, which sought his extradition on human rights charges.

Business & finance

Mar Federal approval of Viagra, anti-impotence pill developed by Pfizer.

Apr Citicorp and Travelers announce merger.

May Daimler-Benz and Chrysler announce merger; largest ever such foreign/US transaction.

Jun Japan in recession, first since 1974.

Aug Russian moratorium on debt; devaluation of the rouble hits hedge fund LTCM (among others), which had huge derivative exposure; international financial meltdown narrowly averted. Critical situation continuing in East Asian economies.

Dec Exxon and Mobil announce merger to make largest global oil company; major restructuring by the second largest, Royal Dutch Shell.

'When I listen to Mozart, the numbers just seem to crunch themselves.'

'It's up to you now, Miller.
The only thing that can save us is an accounting breakthrough.'

'I swear I wasn't looking at smut – I was just stealing music.'

'On the Internet, nobody knows you're a dog.'

'It's not just me, Dad. Amazon.com has never made a cent, either.'

1999

I WAS JUST STEALING MUSIC

Despite (perhaps because of) Federal Reserve Chairman Alan Greenspan's warning of 'irrational exuberance', internet stocks surged in 1999, but gave up all the gain (and more) in the following years. It was a mania in the South Sea Bubble tradition; vast sums were hurled at companies with no more than a concept – most of it was lost. Eighteen-year-old Shawn Fanning dropped out of college to found Napster and soon he had 38 million people exchanging music files to make their own CDs – at $1 a time instead of $15 in the shops. Litigation drove Napster into bankruptcy, but the moguls of the music industry had been shaken to the core; dozens of imitators sprang up and soon pirated CD sales would exceed legitimate sales.

A key ingredient of internet corporate survival is the timing of fundraising. Lastminute.com came to the London stock market in its second year of existence, with no prospect of early earnings, but it still was able to raise £113 million. Although the share price then fell 95%, like so many others, the cash raised at the very top of the market gave lastminute.com a terrific opportunity to build a viable business. The American book retailer, Amazon.com, was able to develop its brilliant business model with the help of its successful fund-raising operations. The vast majority of the new internet companies went down the drain, thereby casting a big cloud over the wider economy, but there was no gainsaying the explosive growth of internet commerce.

AND...

Political & general

Feb President Clinton narrowly averts impeachment over Lewinsky affair.
Mar NATO air strikes force Serbian withdrawal from Kosovo. Resignation of the entire European Commission, amid charges of incompetence, corruption and extravagance.
May Constitutional change in UK with establishment of Scottish Parliament and Welsh Assembly.
Nov Severe disorders at WTO meeting in Seattle; protest groups vent their wrath against the 'global corporate agenda'.
Dec 'Millennium bug' turns out not to be a problem.

Business & finance

Largest ever US visible trade deficit of $347 billion.
Jan Currencies of 11 European countries irrevocably bolted together; UK not involved at this stage.
Jul Privatization of Crédit Lyonnais, after French government had rescued scandal-ridden bank.
Oct WorldCom/Sprint $129 billion merger thwarted by regulators and heavy stock fall.
Nov Gramm-Leach-Bliley Act sweeps away barriers in US banking. Vodafone makes bid for Mannesmann; first major hostile bid of a German company.

'Only time will tell whether this merger makes sense or not.'

2000

THE URGE TO MERGE

There was feverish merger and acquisition activity in 2000; the business had been an Anglo-Saxon preserve but was now a truly global one. Frothing stock markets and the urgings of investment bankers stimulated a host of deals, notably in telecoms, media, pharmaceuticals and banks. Nothing was sacrosanct; the London Stock Exchange itself was embroiled in international merger negotiations. Many deals were plagued by industrial or cultural disaffinities, accentuated by subsequent stock market falls. Shares of the new media group, AOL Time Warner, fell like a stone, which didn't help the merger to bed down.

A particularly sad story was that of General Electric Company, the creation of Arnold Weinstock, Britain's most admired industrialist. After his retirement, GEC sold off dull old makers of cables, weighing machines and medical systems; the money was poured into synchronous digital hierarchy/dense wave multiplexing and other mysterious activities. The company renamed itself after Guglielmo Marconi, the brilliant Italian inventor, who first sent radio signals across the Atlantic; he had said that his inventions were 'for the salvation of humanity' but he would have turned in his grave at the destruction of corporate value done in his name. GEC's £1.5 billion of cash became a debt of £4 billion and the shares fell from £12.50 to a few pence. It was one of many companies to be burned by an irresistible desire for novelty.

AND...

Political & general

Feb Far-right Freedom Party joins ruling coalition in Austria; strains with EU.
Mar Vladimir Putin president of Russia. UK returns General Pinochet to Chile, after judicial process, on health grounds.
Jun Signs of reconciliation between North and South Korea.
Jul President Clinton tries to settle Middle East conflict.
Aug Sinking of Russian nuclear submarine, *Kursk*.
Oct Slobodan Milosevic, Serbian president, loses election; tries to cancel the result, but forced out of office.
Dec After US Supreme Court intervention, George W Bush wins presidential election over Al Gore.

Business & finance

Feb Royal Bank of Scotland acquires National Westminster Bank.
Mar NASDAQ Composite reaches peak, falls 50% by year end – though still at 25 times 1971 level.
May UK mobile phone companies agree to pay £22 billion for new licences.
Jun Microsoft ordered to be broken up.
Jul Crash of Air France's Concorde in Paris.
Sep Danish people reject participation in euro in a referendum.

'And, finally, after a day of record trading on Wall Street,
the entire world was owned by Mickey Mouse.'

'Sotheby's extends its deepest sympathies and wonders whether the deceased might have owned any early German Expressionist pieces.'

'I know more about art than you do, so I'll tell you what to like.'

2001

I'LL TELL YOU WHAT TO LIKE

The dotcom boom might have burnt itself out, but the art market continued to prosper. A measure of its growth was the 200-fold increase in the sales of auctioneers Christie's and Sotheby's over 50 years. From being scholarly boutiques, selling a few pictures or books for the British nobility, they had become behemoths of the art auction business, with an estimated 90% market share and truly global coverage. But they were tempted to break the rules and, in April 2001, had to agree to pay clients $537 million for over-charging them. Sotheby's was also fined $45 million for violating US anti-trust laws. Some of the top people would end up behind bars.

Despite such setbacks, these great old firms survived; people loved the heady mixture of fine art and investment. There was always demand for old masters and Impressionists, but how did you know if a canvas covered in black spots was good or bad art? Or even a hoax or a fraud? There was no way of telling if your $100 outlay might turn into $10,000 or vice versa, and that was half the charm of the market. The golden rule was to buy only what you liked and what you could afford.

AND...

Political & general

Jan Controversial pardons by President Clinton, before inauguration of President George W Bush.

Feb Foot and mouth epidemic in UK; 4 million animals slaughtered, £5.5 billion cost to economy.

Apr US spy plane forced down on Hainan, after collision with Chinese plane; crisis averted by diplomacy.

Jun Tony Blair wins second term after UK election. Mohammed Khatami, reformist leader in Iran, re-elected.

Sep Terrorist attacks in New York and Washington.

Oct USA and allies hit Taleban and Al Qaeda targets in Afghanistan; increased tensions between India and Pakistan. Anthrax attacks in USA.

Business & finance

Feb President Bush proposes $1.6 trillion tax cuts over ten years – largest ever.

Jul GE agreement to buy Honeywell is thwarted by the EU on competition grounds, despite US approvals.

Oct Terrorist attacks reduce global airline income by some 20%; no frills airlines prosper. Bethlehem Steel and other US steel companies in bankruptcy.

Nov China joins WTO in Doha; Taiwan joins one day later.

Dec Financial crisis in Argentina; riots result in deposition of president. Enron, world's largest integrated gas and electricity company, bankrupted after true state of finances revealed.

'OK – let's review what you didn't know and when you didn't know it.'

2002

DELETE THIS E-MAIL

US lawmakers heard of a remarkable exchange between two bankers in July 2002: 'Dollars 5bn in prepays!!!!!!!' and its reply 'Shut up and delete this e mail'. Most people wouldn't know that prepays helped Enron to disguise its debts, but they could certainly smell a rat; it was only a month after Arthur Andersen had shut up shop, having been found guilty of destroying key documents. Enron soon lost its crown as the largest bankruptcy to World-Com, which had overstated profits by $4 billion – later increased to $7 billion and again to $9 billion.

Many a company confessed to similar practices, citing 'generally accepted accounting principles'. Then it turned out that top executives had been hiding their perks; even GE's Jack Welch, America's most admired business leader, had to give up juicy benefits, but only when they were revealed. It didn't help his cause that GE stock was down 50% over two years. Some of the best banks were implicated in monkey business; it was startling to see the name of JP Morgan – banking's classiest name – dragged through the mud. No less startling was the $1.4 billion that the top ten US financial institutions had to pay in penalties for failing to control conflicts of interest – though without admitting guilt.

Widespread illegal and unethical conduct had created a crisis for American capitalism, but a crisis from which its inherent vitality, integrity and wisdom would surely enable it to recover.

AND...

Political & general

Feb Ariel Sharon Prime Minister of Israel; intensified clashes with Palestinians. Milosevic on trial for crimes against humanity at The Hague.
Mar Zimbabwe suspended from Commonwealth.
May Chirac re-elected French president.
Jun After lengthy negotiations, Afghan president Hamid Karzai swears in multi-ethnic cabinet.
Aug US policy to change regime in Iraq.
Sep Earth Summit in Johannesburg.
Nov UN Security Council resolution for Iraq to give up weapons of mass destruction and admit inspectors.

Business & finance

Mar Hotly contested Hewlett-Packard/Compaq merger effective. President Bush announces 30% tariffs to protect US steel industry, despite US commitment to free trade through WTO.
Jun WorldCom largest ever US bankruptcy, total assets being $107 billion.
Jul Sarbanes-Oxley Act passed to curb corrupt practices in US industry and finance.
Dec London house prices at five times their level of 1983.

'Sam, here, is in charge of ethics. He sees that we don't pay out more in bribes than we receive in back-handers.'

'Let's put it this way, Mr Greame: every man's conscience
has its over-ride button.'

'Land ahoy! We have found the New World
and I rename this ship Globalization ...'

GLOBALIZATION'S MILESTONES

Global colonization, trade and industry

1492	Improved ship design enables Christopher Columbus to cross Atlantic in the *Santa Maria* (and return). Beginnings of global trade and colonization from Europe, led by Spain and Portugal. 10 million African slaves cross the Atlantic over the following almost 400 years.
1519–24	First global circumnavigation (Ferdinand Magellan).
1542	St Francis Xavier reaches Goa; global missionary activity accelerates.
1545	Spain's Potosi silver mine in Peru opened; stimulus to global trade, industry and inflation.
1565	Sir John Hawkins introduces tobacco to England.
1600	East India Company set up to promote British global interests (similar Dutch company set up in 1602).
1622	First newspaper in England: *Weekly News*.
1670	Hudson's Bay Company formed to develop Canada.
1689	First packet (post) service from Falmouth to Spain. (New York service came in 1755.)
1694	Bank of England founded; start of large and stable government bond market, a key to Britain's success.
1774–5	James Watt's steam engine and Richard Arkwright's water frame spur UK's industrial revolution.
Late 18th century	40,000 young aristocratic Britons do individual 'Grand Tours' of Europe.
1776	Declaration of Independence – launch of United States of America. UK develops industry and empire; leading global power for next century. Adam Smith's influential espousal of liberal economics and competition, *Wealth of Nations*, published.
1783	First manned flight in balloon by Montgolfier brothers.
1792	UK's envoy, Lord Macartney, attempts to prise open China, but rebuffed.
1804	Sir George Cayley's drawings and models foreshadow modern aeroplane design.
1815 onwards	London becomes leading supplier of global finance.

1810–26	New Latin American nations, formed from Spanish and Portuguese colonies, attract investment.
1811–16	Workers destroy textile machines in protest at potential loss of jobs ('Luddites').
1819	First steam-engine-powered transatlantic crossing. Singapore founded by Stamford Raffles.
1830	Liverpool–Manchester 31-mile railway starts a revolution; travel speeds rise 10-fold and many lands are opened for development (640,000 miles of track globally by 1910).
1831	Michael Faraday's first electric generator.
1833–40	Charles Babbage's analytical engine, prototype computer, helped by UK government funding.
1834–7	Henry Fox Talbot and Louis Daguerre develop photography.
1841	Thomas Cook sets up package tour within England; European and global tourism soon follow.
1843	Opium War; UK and others force their way into China.
1844	Samuel Morse sends first telegram 'What God has wrought' between Baltimore and Washington, USA. Charles Goodyear patents vulcanizing process for rubber; vital for future vehicle industries.
1849	Paul Reuter sends stock market prices by pigeon; founds news agency two years later in London.
1851	First major US foreign investment; Panama Railroad Co. Great Exhibition shows off UK industrial prowess and stimulates competitor nations.
1857	After mutiny, UK consolidates its direct rule in India.
1859	Edwin Drake starts oil industry at Titusville, USA.
1863	Discovery of germ theory permits improvements in public health. Henri Dunant founds Red Cross to give cross-border relief for victims of war and disaster.
1865–1914	After Civil War, USA becomes largest industrial power. Germany, France, Italy, Russia and Japan challenge UK's global leadership.
1865	First international organization – International Telegraph (now Telecommunication) Union.
1866	IK Brunel's *Great Eastern* steamship lays transatlantic telegraph cable after several false starts.

'Miss Boxfile, you may relax. The computer menace would appear to have been greatly exaggerated.'

1867	Karl Marx's *Das Kapital* predicts the end of capitalism.
1868	Foreign & Colonial Investment Trust set up as collective vehicle for investors of 'moderate means'.
1869	Suez Canal opened.
1870	John D Rockefeller starts Standard Oil Company and develops monopoly.
1870–1910	13% of Europe's workers emigrate to New World to better themselves.
1871	First transatlantic liner, *Oceanic* (the liner trade lasted about 100 years).
1873	Christopher Sholes and Carlos Glidden's first commercial typewriter, made by Remington.
1874	Universal Postal Union formed.
1876	Alexander Graham Bell invents telephone.

1880s	First electric lighting (Swan and Edison) and motor cars (Daimler and Benz).
1885	Congress of Berlin regulates African colonization; the 'scramble for Africa'.
1886	Dr John Pendleton invents Coca-Cola.
1890	US census mechanized by Herman Hollerith (his company later becomes IBM).
1895	Lumière Brothers set up first cinema. First use of X-rays for medical purposes.
1896	First modern Olympic Games; ideal of uniting peoples of the world through friendly rivalry.
1901	Guglielmo Marconi sends first transatlantic radio signals.
1903	Wright Brothers make first manned aeroplane flight. Henry Ford starts car mass-production.
1911	Fall of Manchu regime in China; more foreign intrusion and influence.
1914	British global influence at zenith; holds 41% of international investments. Panama Canal opened.

Two global wars and their aftermath

1914–39	WWI, followed by recession, revolution and decolonization, holds back globalization.
1917	Russian Revolution; new Soviet Union independent of global economy.
1919	First transatlantic flight (Alcock and Brown).
1920s	Start of radio broadcasting, commercial air transport and international phone calls.
1930s	Development of computers.
1932	Launch of BBC Empire News (later World Service), renowned as impartial global broadcaster.
1939	19,000 TV sets in UK and fewer than 1,000 in USA (over one billion globally today).
1939–40	Increased use of antibiotics, such as Alexander Fleming's penicillin (discovered 1928).
1939–45	WWII stimulates technology, especially in USA (aviation, electronics, computers, radio, TV).
1944–6	United Nations, World Bank and IMF formed; US dollar supremacy for next 25 years.

1946–75	Vietnam War (between Hanoi regime and France, to 1954, then USA).
1946–89	Cold War; Western democracies against Soviet bloc, with some involvement of China.
1946 onwards	British and other empires hasten decolonization.
1947	USA launches Marshall Plan to reconstruct Europe and rebuilds Japan.
	General Agreement on Tariffs and Trade (GATT) set up to promote free trade.
	Invention of transistor.
1949	Mao Tse-tung proclaims People's Republic of China; foreign influences expelled.

Accelerating globalization

| 1950 onwards | Export-led recovery of Japan, Germany and Italy after defeats in WWII. |
| 1951 | US Census Bureau's new computer weighs 18 tons. |

'Of course, every village has got its Global Village Idiot nowadays.'

181

1951 cont.	Three-minute phone call New York to London costs $73 (in 2002 dollars); now 20 cents or less, one main supplier replaced by 50 suppliers today.
1952	SS *United States* makes record Atlantic crossing (3 days, 17 hours, 48 mins).
1953	First commercial jet airliner, Comet, crashes four times.
1954	First US commercial jet airliner, Boeing 707 (6 hours New York to London). Passenger air miles rise 40 fold and freight air miles 80 fold by 2000.
about 1955	Eurocurrency market starts ($10 trillion today).
1957	European Economic Community formed by 6 nations.
1958	Invention of silicon chip (capacity rises by factor of 125 million over next 40 years).
1959	UK and 6 nations form European Free Trade Area. First case of AIDS in Congo; becomes global disease – over 40 million affected today.
1961	Typical computer with peripherals costs $2 million (equivalent today below $1,000).
1962	TELSTAR launched, permitting transatlantic TV broadcasts. Cuban Missile Crisis nearly triggers nuclear war between USA and Soviet Union. Marshall McLuhan writes that electronic interdependence makes world 'a global village'.
1963	US capital controls stimulate Eurobond issues ($100 million, rising to $1.2 trillion today).
1964	Escalation of Vietnam War; reduced dollar confidence.
1965	Moore's Law – transistor capacity doubles yearly, leading to miniaturization of components and massive computer economies. Cross-border lending begins to expand rapidly ($2.3 billion rising to $1.5 trillion today).
1970	Boeing 747 increases air travel capacity; end of transatlantic liner trade.
1971	Devaluation of dollar; end of post-war currency regime. Agitation from oil producers for better terms. First micro-processors, leading to personal computers (over 600 million today).
1971–80	OECD cross-border investment annual average $30 billion ($1 trillion today).

'Smaller, more powerful chips allow me to have a smaller head.'

1972	President Nixon visits China and Soviet Union in pursuit of détente.
	Financial futures start in Chicago ($100 trillion today).
	Daily foreign exchange turnover $72 billion ($1.5 trillion today).
	ARPANET launched, precursor of the internet (650 million users today).
1973	First oil shock; surge and spread of global lending, by factor of 8 in 7 years. Arab investors active around the globe.

1976	Genentech formed, pioneer biotechnology company.
	After death of Mao Tse-tung, China liberalizes.
	First supersonic commercial jet flights by Concorde
	(New York to London in 3 hours).
1979	Second oil shock, following Iranian revolution.
	Soviet invasion of Afghanistan.
1979 and 1981	Thatcher and Reagan in power, promote globalization.
1980	First mobile phones (one billion today).
	Start of CNN, global TV service (200 countries today).
1980s	Democracy and free markets come to South America.
1982–7	Third World debt crisis; debt/equity swaps lead to rise
	of emerging market equities.
1985–9	Surge in Japanese foreign investment, built on huge
	trade surplus.
1985	Mikhail Gorbachev in power; major changes in Soviet
	Union.
1989	'Washington Consensus' to promote universal free
	markets.
1989–91	Fall of the Soviet Union; independence for satellites.
1991	Market economy in Russia and Eastern Europe brings
	Marxism to an end.
	Tim Berners-Lee invents World Wide Web (www),
	leading to global spread of internet use.
1994	MERCOSUR and NAFTA trade bodies to promote free
	trade in the Americas.
1995	World Trade Organization (WTO) replaces GATT.
1997	WTO seeks accelerated liberalization of global financial
	service markets.
1997–8	East Asian and Russian crises test validity of liberal
	capitalist model.
1999	Mounting protests against corporate globalization;
	prime targets WTO and IMF.
2000	Record year for cross-border mergers.
2001	9/11 outrages; President Bush's global war on terror.
2001–2	Corporate and accounting scandals erode confidence.

'Know what really chokes me?
That £50,000 computer I stole now sells for £69.95.'

ACKNOWLEDGEMENTS

I am grateful to Nick Roberts, Brigitte Istim and Helen Walasek at *Punch* and Andy Pillsbury and Richard Madigan at the *New Yorker*. Without their unfailing help and enthusiasm, this book would never have seen the light of day. All but eleven of the cartoons were originally published in these two magazines (see below for the exceptions) and I am greatly indebted to them for permission to reproduce.

I am also indebted to the *Sun* for permission to reproduce Stanley Franklin's cartoon about the Falklands (page 108), and to David Langdon, Orion Story Limited, and Thomson Financial, publishers of *IFR* magazine, for permission to reproduce two of David's cartoons (pages 48 and 130 respectively). David also produced two cartoons expressly for this book (pages vi and 176). The four cartoons by Osbert Lancaster (pages 8, 26, 76 and 179) are reproduced with permission of John Murray. I am grateful to Nicholas Garland for permission to reproduce the cartoon on page 129, originally published in the *Independent*, and to Ingram Pinn and the *Financial Times* for permission to reproduce the back cover cartoon.

Andrew Franklin and Paul Forty of my publishers, Profile Books, have been wonderfully patient and supportive in the creation of this book. Fiona Screen has been an assiduous and expert copy-editor. I have received a lot of help from Anna Thomas and Jane Newton of the University of Kent; its department for the study of cartoons and related website have been quite invaluable to me. I owe thanks to my family and friends who made comments on the book as it evolved.

Finally, my thanks go to John Langton of International Securities Market Association for showing an enthusiastic and supportive interest in the book's earliest stages.